Survival Kit
for the Stranded

Helps for Those Who Hurt

Carolyn Shealy Self and William L. Self

Ministerial Association
General Conference of Seventh-day Adventists

Scripture marked RSV is taken from the Revised Standard Version of the Bible. Copyright © 1946, 1952, 1971, by the Division of Christian Education of the National Council of Churches in the U.S.A. Used by permission.

Copyright © 1998
Ministerial Association
General Conference of Seventh-day Adventists

Originally published by Broadman Press in 1975.
All copy has been reset and repaginated.

PRINTED IN U.S.A.
Pacific Press® Publishing Association
Nampa, ID 83687

ISBN 1-57847-021-8

We lovingly dedicate this book to those who are still trying to survive being stranded with us: our patient parents; our children, Lee and Bryan; our dear friend and secretary, Dorothy Reeves; and the understanding people of the Wieuca Road Baptist Church.

Foreword

I'm tired of easy answers. You know, those simple, slick answers given by those who are insensitive to human need. They have neither hurt enough, cried enough, nor doubted enough to help us.

I'm not impressed by those who have all the answers to give. Somehow, their glib easiness only reinforces my pain. A Jeremiah weeping with me; a Job crying out against life's injustice; or Jesus, with the demanding honesty of Psalm 22—"My God, my God, why . . ." speak more to my pain than the current crop of insensitive "double knit clad" answer givers. They demand only that we acknowledge their success.

Granted that there are answers—and granted that the old cliches do have meaning underneath their smooth edges—but after twenty years in the practice of ministry I'm convinced that most of us need something to help us survive until things change . . . until we can work the situation through. We need this more than answers. What we need is a survival kit that will give us life until help arrives.

These pages recognize the human situation and offer a few handles to hang onto until help comes.

Bill Self

Contents

Introduction   7

Stranded with Grief   9
    Bill

Stranded with Guilt   19
    Carolyn and Bill

Stranded with Fear   27
    Bill

Stranded in Illness   35
    Carolyn and Bill

Stranded in Mental Illness   47
    Carolyn

Stranded Alone   63
    Bill

Stranded with Despair   75
    Bill

Stranded in the Middle   83
    Bill

Stranded Parents   93
    Carolyn and Bill

Stranded in the Stained-Glass Jungle   105
    Carolyn

Stranded at the End   119
    Bill

How to Survive: True Faith and True Grit   127
    Carolyn and Bill

Afterthought   134

Introduction

One year on a Memorial Day weekend our family took advantage of the school holiday and went to a secluded spot in the north Georgia mountains, Sky Valley. The cottages are built on the side of the mountain, the lodge is in the valley below. From our cottage on the side of the mountain, we could see everything that went on below. We saw the cars coming and going, the tractors and the bulldozers working on the golf course, people swimming and playing tennis, and surrounding it were the shadows on the mountains. It was a delightful weekend and we decided that Bill, my husband, would leave Bryan, our youngest son, and me there while he returned to Atlanta Saturday night to preach on Sunday. He would join us again Sunday night after the evening service.

Sunday was a beautiful day. Bryan had a friend visiting him for the weekend and about mid-afternoon his parents came for him. Bryan and I were left alone with no transportation.

About four o'clock the sky began to get dark and we had a little rain. Later on, the wind began to blow and the rain came down hard and fast. Later we found out that it had rained seven inches in five hours. We saw the other week-enders leaving and began to feel rather isolated.

We heard that a tornado had hit the power station at Tallulah Falls not far away. The thunder and lightning cracked all around us. We couldn't leave because we had no car, and by now the clay road was like a river. Since we had no choice, we had to wait it out. I was worried about my husband coming back. I knew he would leave Atlanta about nine o'clock, and the weather reports sounded as if he would be driving right in the path of the storm. I couldn't reach him by phone, and I knew he would be as worried about us as we were about him.

I walked the floor and prayed for protection for all of us. I kept looking out the window, watching for car lights to come into the valley. About twelve midnight I saw him coming. I knew he couldn't drive the car up the mountain road to us because, through the flashes of lightning, I could see that the road had become a river. I thought he'd stop at the lodge and the night watchman would tell him not to drive up. Sure enough I saw the lights of the car stop at the lodge, and I was relieved—everything would be all right. But then to my dismay, I saw the car lights move again starting up the road. As Bill approached the bend where the creek goes under the road, I saw the front car lights go down and under water and then the tail lights went out.

My heart stopped beating, I'm sure. In the flashes of lightning, I saw that the whole front end of the station wagon was under water and I didn't know if Bill had gotten out or not. Finally, I could see the figure of one man moving around and I couldn't tell if it were the night watchman or my husband. I can't describe my feelings.

Bryan was very courageous and helpful even though I'm sure he must have been terribly upset over having an hysterical mother and perhaps a drowned father. Finally, we saw the beam of a flashlight coming up the ski slope, and I ran out in the mud and rain to see if it was the night watchman with death news—or my husband. My heart nearly burst with joy and thankfulness to hear Bill's voice calling to me. The watchman had not realized how deep the creek water had become and had told Bill he could drive up.

When the wagon went in, it sank up to the front seat and Bill couldn't open the doors. He had to climb out the tail gate. Needless to say that car is no longer part of our family. The storm raged on through the night. The next morning was clear and sunny, and again we thanked God for keeping us safe and together. We were no longer stranded.

We had been physically alone that stormy night and realized that there are many types of storms that leave people stranded.

We hope that this book will provide you with a survival kit for the times when you feel stranded.

Carolyn Self

Stranded with Grief
Bill

*D*o you remember the old nursery rhyme that the children used to recite? It went: "Hark, hark, the dogs do bark, the beggars are coming to town, / Some in rags and some in tags and some in velvet gowns."

Somehow I think that we have to be honest with ourselves and come to grips with the fact that all of us are hiding some grief underneath velvet gowns, manicured lawns, beautiful automobiles, and mink stoles. These do not cover the deepest pain of life, and let's understand that.

Some grieve because they never knew their fathers; others grieve because they did. Some grieve because they have never made it in their chosen profession; others grieve because they have made it and have found that it's empty, and they stand at the peak of their profession and, like Peggy Lee in song cries out: "Is that all there is?" Some grieve because they never had children; others grieve because they did. Some grieve because they miss the hometown, the neighborhood school, the high school football days, being a cheerleader, and lost youth, and those days can never come again.

Others, like old all-Americans, look over their shoulders and, fondling their trophies one more time, realize that baldness and grayness and stooping shoulders must come to all. Some grieve because they have left home; others grieve because they can't. But whatever it is that causes your heart to be heavy, whatever the situation may be, the church ought to be a place where people can come together and grieve.

Early in my ministry I preached a sermon on the subject of grief because my people were going through some heavy difficulties. Later in the week I was confronted by a gentleman who had heard the sermon and was livid with anger. With fierce emotion in his eyes, he looked at me and said: "The church is no place for anybody to talk about grief." I finally realized that the sermon had activated his unresolved grief concerning the death of his mother several years before. I think my friend did not understand the truth of the Spanish philosopher, Unamuno, when he observed: "The proper use of a Temple is to provide a place where people can grieve together."

If the church is going to be anything, it must be a place where we can come together and bring our sorrows and griefs. In fact, as I looked at the Old and New Testaments, I was overwhelmed with the fact that we talk about Jesus, the man who was acquainted with our grief, who has borne our sorrows.

We talk about the Holy Spirit as the Comforter of God. We talk about our not being ignorant about those who are departed. The New Testament is clear with its understanding that God gives comfort to those who go through difficult places. But in the stupidity of twentieth-century America, we have a crazy kind of idea that people are never supposed to show their emotions. If anything ever goes wrong in your life, don't ever tell anybody. The idea that church is a collection of people who have been victors in life is wrong. It's not even Christian.

I get terribly concerned with people who seem to think that because life has dealt them a body blow, they can't come back to the household of faith. I would that all of us could attend church dressed in rags one Sunday so that we could have out in the open what we're trying to hide inside.

Grief is a universal experience. You're thinking: I haven't lost anybody; there have been no funerals at my house lately. That may be true, and you may somehow think you're immune. You may live in a big house that's half paid for. You may command a salary that's greater than you deserve. You may have an incredibly good education and you may be getting great advancement in business. I am not only talking about those who have lost loved ones in that ultimate difficulty called death, but most of us hide things that are so deep we cannot utter them anyway.

I want the church to come to grips with the fact that the church ought to be a place where we can be honest enough to grieve together. You may grieve because there's no feeling in your life. You may grieve because there's too much. But all of us go through it. There are various stages of it.

All of this is enough to drive us to despair, to drugs, to drink in order to forget our minks and automobiles. All of this, when we come to realize the heavy load of pain that most people carry, is enough to make us like Job, thinking about cursing God and dying. When ultimate loss and separation come into a life, as Granger Westburg has noted in his book *Good Grief,* there are several approaches that people use in attempting to handle grief.

First of all, when a person realizes grief has come, there is a sense of *shock.* "I can't go on. I can't believe it." Then there's a sense of *emotional relief* when maybe tears or laughter or another kind of emotional expression breaks through. Then there's the third stage when people begin to feel terribly *depressed, isolated, cut off.* Sometimes physical symptoms move in. One study I read indicated that 38 percent of the people in a certain hospital were patients who had suffered a significant loss prior to their hospitalization. Then the fourth stage is a *sense of guilt.* Someone says, "If only I had done this" or "If only we had done that, then this would not have happened." The fifth stage is a *sense of anger.* People do not always follow this uniformly, but there's a sense of anger when you reach out. The doctor is wrong, I'm mad at him; or the church didn't do something and I'm mad at it. Something is wrong; in anger you reach out and fight at the world for what's happened to you. The last stage is a *sense of hope* where the cloud breaks and hope emerges. You begin to understand what Paul meant when he said: "Grieve, but not as men who have no hope."

As Christian people in a Christian community, we grieve as those who do have hope, for you see we've learned that the gospel moves in at a time of need. Look in the Old Testament, and you realize that when heavy grief moved upon the people of Israel, God took them out of their bondage. You look in and see that when Job, brokenhearted and his body filled with sores, sat on the ash heap, God came in and gave him a sense of hope. When Jeremiah wept over a country that he had lost, God moved in and gave him a sense of hope. When Isaiah was weeping over the burdens and sorrows of the Israelites, he came to the place where he was able to utter that magnificent cry, "Surely he will bear our sorrows."

And Luke, the talented physician, understands God in the ultimate way in Jesus Christ when he can say: "He came to heal the brokenhearted." And I would say in parentheses: "Not to congratulate the successful, but to heal the broken-hearted." And the early Christian community echoed Paul: "We would not have you ignorant, brethren, concerning those who are asleep, that ye may not grieve as others do who have no hope."

You see, the Christian is not immune from grief, but the Christian wants to turn bad grief into good grief. The Christian wants to go through the stages of grief with hope. The Christian wants to pass through the pain of grief with understanding that there's more out there than the emptiness—the empty room. There's more there than the emptiness of a life where relationships have been severed. The Christian goes through this with an understanding that God has not abandoned him. I want you to view grief not as ultimate pain but, hopefully, in a Christian stance as opportunity.

It is difficult in the grief experience to recognize any good at all. Sometimes it is only in a crucial situation like grief that the depths of our personal, inner resources are tapped. We never know the strength and sureness of our faith until we have to search our very souls and measure our ability to cope with this situation. It is like a general in the army who really never can tell how disciplined and well trained his troops are until the battle is raging. Grief can either conquer you or push you forward into new frontiers of personal growth.

Ten years ago when we first moved to Atlanta, my mother came from Florida to visit a prominent surgeon here. As we were in his office for a few hours, I had the opportunity of talking to this man. I noted his gentleness and understanding as he dealt with my mother. There seemed to be an unusual dimension in the compassion of this man. I learned later how brutalized his life had been by the tragic death of his teenage son in a boating accident. He had gone through the stages of adjustment and had come through with a new and deeper compassion for people, particularly his patients. Those who talked with him through this tragedy and supported him through his grief knew that he had dealt with his pain through his strong faith and had "made it"—not as an embittered man still asking, "Why me, Lord?" but with a beautiful spirit of caring.

Since that time, I have looked at other people who have gone through the ultimate of life's crushing blows—and there was a time when I would say this glibly as an orator in the pulpit. I say it now as a man who has stood by too many open graves, too many broken marriages, too many crushed lives and wrecked careers. I've seen too many kids on drugs, I've seen too many of you who are crying, "Is that all there is?" to say it glibly.

But I want you to know you're not worth much until your heart's been broken. I don't believe God can do anything with a man until his heart has been broken. Until you're a bruised reed, you don't mean anything to life.

I heard one of the greatest orators I've ever heard stand in a pulpit and deliver a magnificent sermon. The man put together words in a marvelous fashion; his use of the Scripture was sheer brilliance; his weaving together of thoughts and ideas was something to behold. It was a masterpiece. There was only one thing wrong with it. The man was wrapped in cellophane wrap. I *saw* him but never *felt* him. I felt he could never reach out and get to me. He protected himself completely. There was not one drop of blood in it.

I'll take the unlettered, inarticulate man whose heart has been plowed under by the heaviness of life and has found God in the darkness to tell me about God. Now I say to you; you're not worth anything until your heart's been broken, and I hope this is some sense of comfort for the brokenhearted. You don't go out and ask for these things to come, but you understand this does not mean the end or defeat. It means that grief develops within you a sensitivity that gives you the ability to understand and to deal with life. The cold-hearted, manipulative manager who is able to go through life and keep it in perfect order is one thing, but the bruised and bleeding reed who has the hope of God in his heart may not have everything in proper perspective as far as keeping the minutia of life controlled, but he has a depth and touch and feeling in his life that projects like nothing else.

Harry Emerson Fosdick, perhaps the greatest preacher of the first half of this century, wrote a significant book called *The Meaning of Prayer*. It's still a classic on prayer. Fosdick noted after the book had become a publishing triumph that he never could have written the book if he had not suffered a nervous breakdown early in his ministry and gone through some of the most difficult periods of his life. He said the book came out of his nervous breakdown.

Rollo May, a notable author in the area of mental illness and pastoral care, pointed out that our best work never comes in the moment of our triumph, but our best work comes out of the valleys, out of pain, out of tension, out of agony. May indicated that no one produces anything of any significance until he has walked the deep areas and has gone through the suffering places.

"Grieve," Paul says, "but not as men who have no hope." And for the Christian community we say, here we are with all of our griefs. They're out on the surface. We don't have to apologize about them. We don't have to tell the world they're not there. We can acknowledge them. That's why in the Christian community when one is broken, the others go there because we know his pain, but we also know God is working with him. That's why we come together to sing the praises of God, because there's a hope beyond what we have. We come together understanding that God walks through whatever life brings, and he walks triumphantly with us.

We gather not as broken men who line the highways of our city, but as triumphant men and women, knowing that God is there. We come to hear the voice of the Old Testament, "Underneath are the everlasting arms of God." We come with the hope of the New Testament which says that before us is an open tomb, and we have given testimony to it in our own lives.

Grief comes into our lives in many ways. Grieving over the death of a loved one is all-consuming, whether the death has come as a result of long illness, accident, or suicide. Death, however, is not the only legitimate cause of grief.

Consider the divorced person who endures a severed relationship and yet experiences continued exposure to the "deceased" through the children.

Consider the torment of guilt and grief experienced by the family of a person convicted of a hideous crime.

The anguish and grief of the family circle of an alcoholic or a drug addict is a continual festering sore.

A middle-aged man grieving over his devastated career goals is almost inconsolable and feels inadequate in all areas.

Each person, each unit of grief, has to cope in some way with his situation. This comes by meeting grief head-on—not by trying to escape or ignore it. Many a person, while running away from grief, structures his whole life to accommodate this way of coping. There always a time, somewhere in the future, when this unresolved grief has to be explored and dealt with.

Grief comes to all people everywhere. Grief comes to the rich, middle class, and poor. Grief is a common denominator—not success, not failure.

I wish that I had some kind of spiritual solvent that could wash away those protective veneers that most of us have erected. I wish we could wash them away so we could see the rich grain of our lives. I wish we could peel them off so we could see not the veneer that you've worked so hard to put there, but the rich, warm grain of your life. Sometimes God does that when he tells us that we must go through the valley that is so filled with shadows. Catherine Marshall in *To Live Again* talks about how God took the clouds away from her life after she had been in the midst of what could be the darkest hour of her life.

One of my favorite authors, Thomas Wolfe, in one of his novels tells almost autobiographically of a six-foot, ten-inch author named George Weber who was struggling in New York City and to whom the dry periods would come. Every writer, preacher, thinker passes through these dry periods of creativity. He could not get anything to come, and he would get on a train and take an overnight ride all the way down to the mountains of North Carolina where his mother lived. He would walk up to the old cabin, go up on the porch, and every time his mother would be there to greet him. He would sit down on the top step there on the porch of that cabin and the big gangling writer would put his head in the lap of his understanding old mother and she'd put her hand on his shoulder. He wouldn't say anything and she wouldn't say anything, but they would just rock together there.

She presently would articulate words like: "George, it's going to be all right; whatever it is, it's going to be all right." George Weber would spend twenty-four to forty-eight hours with his mother in that old cabin, and then he would take the train back to New York.

I think somehow that's what the church ought to be. The church of the Lord Jesus Christ ought to be a place where we can come and grieve together. It ought to be a temple where we as a fellowship of faith can gather and put our heads in the lap of the Lord Jesus and rock awhile and let him put those nail-scarred hands on our shoulders and say: "It's going to be all right. I know what it is and I've come to give comfort."

To those of you who do not find a supportive fellowship

of love and care in your present situation, perhaps you should search diligently for the church where you, as part of the community of faith, can both support and be supported. Perhaps part of your unresolved grief is the bitterness that goes with feeling excluded from a loving family and community.

You need to feel the loving compassion of the nail-scarred hand pulling you up and to hear the words, "It's going to be all right."

Grieve. Go ahead and grieve. Get it out. Cry it out. Whatever it may be. It may be literal death, or it may be one of those other circumstances I alluded to. Go ahead and do it; but don't do it as though you had no hope, for you remember that the church touches life not in its superficial dimensions but where it is the hardest and the heaviest—at birth, at death, at conversion.

Remember that when God talks to the church, he says things like: "He was despised and rejected by men. He was a man of sorrow, acquainted with grief." As one from whom men hide their faces, "He was despised and we esteemed him not. Surely he has borne our grief and carried our sorrows. Yet we esteemed him stricken, smitten by God and afflicted, but he was wounded for our transgressions; he was bruised for our iniquities; upon him was the chastisement that made us whole. With his stripes we are healed." Grieve. Let it flow. Tell God about it. Grieve but not as those who are without hope. The church, the proper use of the temple, is to make it a place where men can grieve together.

Stranded With Guilt

Carolyn

*I*t is an accepted fact that illness, both physical and mental, can occasionally be traced to the patient's feeling of guilt and unworthiness. This was brought out very dramatically to me with a patient who was my primary responsibility as a therapist. This young woman, in hoping to be popular, had gone the route of drug abuse, prostitution, had undergone an abortion recently, and in earlier years had given up for adoption a baby born out of wedlock. She had been treated very cruelly and had been used and abused by men. We talked as often as she desired every day. Many times she would stop in mid-sentence, call herself a derogatory term, and walk away. She frequently asked to go to the chapel and to see a minister. We had no chapel building on the grounds and it took awhile for her to accept me, a woman, as a chaplain. The whole staff made an effort to take every opportunity to affirm Betsy. We could see some improvement, but she just couldn't believe that we could like her just for herself.

One day she came to my office and said, "I need to talk." I will give you a brief summary of our conversation.

Betsy: Carolyn, do you really like me?
Counselor: You know I do, Betsy.
Betsy (sobbing): I don't like myself. I'm ashamed of myself. I hate myself, and I feel so guilty about what I've done to my parents. My mom tried to tell me. They wanted me to be good and I wouldn't even listen. I was so mean and ugly to them. I thought those boys would like me, and every time I thought one would marry me, but they just kicked me around and called me horrible names. Now nobody wants me, and I don't

blame them.

Counselor: Go ahead and cry all you want. Betsy, remember how you've been asking for a chapel and a minister? (She nods yes.) Why do you feel the need for that?

Betsy: I just wondered what I can do so God will forgive me.

Counselor: You don't need a chapel or a minister for that, Betsy. All you need to do is to tell God yourself that you are sorry about the way you've lived and behaved; ask him to forgive you and he will.

Betsy: Can we do that now? (She got down on her knees by my desk—I was surprised—but quickly knelt beside her. She reached for my hand and I held it tightly.)

Counselor: Would you like for me to pray first? (She nodded yes.) "Dear Father, Betsy is so burdened with the guilt she has about the way she has misused this precious life you have given her. Now, Father, I love Betsy and her family loves her and we all want so much for her to be well and strong again. Please forgive her for her past sins and let her feel your forgiveness and your loving care. Thank you for making this forgiveness possible through Jesus. Amen."

Betsy: "Dear God, I am sorry (and she lists many things). Please forgive me and help me not to be that way anymore. Bless Carolyn and the nurses and doctors. Amen."

When we finished, she was not rigid and tense anymore. We talked a few more minutes, and I reminded her of the incident of Jesus asking water of the Samaritan woman whom everybody shunned because of her sinful life and how he forgave her and changed her life. I made her promise to quit calling herself ugly names and as she left, she smiled and hugged me and said, "I feel so much better now."

I am happy to say that Betsy improved, slowly but surely.

This is one type of guilt—easily recognizable. There are other kinds of guilt that can be just as devastating. Betsy's parents were carrying a heavy load of guilt—beating themselves daily with questions of what they could have done differently.

Sometimes mothers feel guilty when they sneak time to read a book or pamper themselves instead of wielding the mop or baking cookies. Fathers feel guilty because their work demands so much time away from the family, but they would also feel guilty if they were unable to provide for the needs of the family. Working mothers can feel very guilty, but when it is necessary (either for money or personal fulfillment) most children are quite able to adjust. Children feel guilty when they are not able to win the coveted scholarship or trophy for parents to brag about. Friends and relatives make us feel guilty when we do not visit them often enough.

There are times when our consciences need to be pricked into acute awareness of our problem areas. That doesn't mean that we are left stranded, holding an ever increasing load of guilt. That old gospel song says it well: "Take your burden to the Lord and *leave* it there."

Bill

Let's talk about how to survive when you're stranded with an overwhelming sense of guilt. In Genesis 3:10 there is an interesting conversation between God and Adam. Adam had fallen into sin, yielded to the temptation; and God came back through the garden, as he was accustomed to doing and he called out. This conversation took place: "The Lord God called unto Adam and said unto him, Where art thou?" "And he said, I heard thy voice in the garden, and I was afraid, because I was naked; and I hid myself." "And he said, Who told thee that thou wast naked? Hast thou eaten of the tree, whereof I commanded thee that thou shouldest not eat?"

This is the first recorded incident of someone experiencing guilt and guilt causing him to do things he normally would not have done. I try when people come to see me, as any other professional would, to protect their identity and protect what they have to say because I feel as though that is a very sacred time. But there have been overwhelming times when I've talked to people and have been impressed with the fact they're being driven by a sense of guilt.

I remember a young lady who sat in my office a good while ago. Frankly, she was overdressed and over made up and she seemed to be compensating for a lot of things that either were or were not in her life. The more she talked, the more I was convinced that if it could be done in the city of Atlanta, she had done it. And then she told me how this had made her feel. She looked at me and the tears were beginning to come from the corners of her eyes, her mascara was beginning to run, and her eyelashes were becoming entangled, and she blurted out, "Do you really believe that God can forgive me for the things that I have done?" We talked awhile and as we continued to talk, I realized that all she really wanted was a sense of being forgiven for her sins.

There is one edge that the professional clergy who engage in counseling have over the other professional disciplines in this area. I mention this in broad, general terms, knowing, of course, that theologically I probably can't support this. But in the public mind, the clergy can forgive men. Now I know the Catholic clergy is supposed to do that. We only point to One who does forgive, but we are in contact with the root source of forgiveness in this world.

This young lady looked at me and said that the sense of guilt was there. We prayed intensely together. As she left, I could tell that some weights had been lifted. She said: "You know, God has forgiven me."

Then, there was a divorcee who came to see me. She continued to tell me about the burden she was carrying. It developed that the thing really bothering her was that she felt unclean because she had been involved in a marriage that didn't make it.

She explained: "I am a Christian." She continued to tell me about how active she had been and how meaningful her Christian life had been, but she confessed, "I don't feel acceptable any longer because of this experience in my life." I asked her if she had confessed this to God, and she replied: "I have, but I still can't get any sense of freedom about it."

Finally, I looked at her and said the very obvious thing: "God has already forgiven you. Forgiveness is not cheap with God, but he forgave you at Calvary and you have appropriated that forgiveness for your own life. But you haven't forgiven yourself." She answered: "You're right, I have not forgiven myself."

All of us who deal with people who are carrying burdens and who are plagued by a sense of guilt encounter a large percentage of people who never forgive themselves. They spend their lives flailing themselves for something they've done wrong. They carry guilt in their lives that God never intended for them to carry. And I think our churches are at fault at this point. I really believe the churches have mistakenly gotten caught on the guilt bandwagon.

Several years ago there was a young lady in our church who married and moved to another community. She came to our church from a church that played on her guilt all the time. That church loaded its members up with guilt. They simply backed their wagons up to the church and loaded them up with guilt every Sunday morning and night. After being in our services, she said, "When are you going to make me feel bad?" I replied, "Well, you come in January when I start raising the budget and you'll feel awful." She asked: "What do I do between now and then? I'm enjoying this church. I feel bad because I feel good in church."

I tried to help her see that the church is the body of Christ. Christ spent his time forgiving people; Christ devoted himself to lifting the load of guilt; Christ ministered by affirming people. The only people that Christ had harsh words for were those religious people who were so tight on the inside they couldn't love and forgive and affirm.

If you're carrying a load of guilt, remember that the conscience is a monitor of God on human actions. I've read article after article on the conscience. I'm not really happy with anything I've read, but I believe we can go with this statement: *The conscience is the monitor of God on human actions*. I'm aware that you can condition your conscience. I've met people who have no conscience. They can drown little kittens and never have any problems with that. They can push people down stairs, get in front of you in line—you know, nothing ever bothers them. They've conditioned their conscience not even to quiver.

There are some people who have a conscience so overdeveloped they can't move or bat an eye without having a pang of conscience. But somewhere between these two extremes is a healthy balance. If you have a little twinge of guilt now and then for things you've said or done, or a good, healthy push of guilt or a pain of guilt, that's not all bad.

Christ frees us from this unreasonable sense of guilt. I think if the truth were known, most of us actually don't feel as though we're the kind of persons we ought to be. We have all of these blinders put on us and all of these limitations that we have imposed upon ourselves, because we've convinced ourselves we're not good.

This summer we were walking through the churches in Europe—even when I'm not preaching in one, I want to walk in every one I see—and we were in a village in France, Les Houches, where at the foot of Mont Blanc was a little church right out in the middle of the street.

The street encircled the church and I said to my family: "Let's go in." And they said: "Another church?" I encouraged them: "Sure, you know we haven't seen this one." They agreed with obvious lack of enthusiasm. It was a dimly lit church. It was at twilight and visibility was difficult and our eyes had not yet adjusted to the darkness—semi-darkness.

As we paused and looked around the musty old church, the boys spied some little black booths along the wall. "What are those cabinets for?" they wanted to know. "Those are the confessionals," I replied. And I explained to them how in the Roman Church there is a confessional where the priest is on one side and the penitent is on the other and they talk and the penitent confesses his sins. Then one of the boys looked at me and asked: "Is that about like counseling?" And I honestly believe he was right.

I think the Protestant equivalent to this is pastoral care,

whether it's done in a pastor's office or in some other type of clinical experience. If you're carrying an unreasonable load of guilt—and if you have about you enough balance to understand that this thing which is breaking your back or breaking your heart is a sense of guilt over whatever it is that has transpired, real or imagined—find someone to tell it to. But make sure the one to whom you tell it is responsible, a professional. Don't tell it to the village gossip or to someone who cannot wait to share it with your boss.

You can't carry it in your soul, and God gave us one another to help carry those burdens. The Scriptures say: "Cast your burdens on the Lord." Tell God about it and even tell intimate, personal friends or a professional—meaning clergy or a professional counselor—to rid yourself of that kind of weight.

There are those who think that telling it is to admit some kind of weakness. There is this stupid idea that sort of permeates our society: "Oh, I can't ask for help; that will admit there's something wrong with me." If you're a human being and if you have blood in your veins and skin on your bones, there's something wrong with you. If your leg was broken out there in the street, we'd get you to the hospital and to the doctor quickly; and we'd all rush in and celebrate the fact that we got some help for you. But if your heart is broken, you put up a good front—everything's perfect with me—and your heart is caving in inside.

Now forgive yourself. That's right. Don't be harder on yourself than God is. I'm not making light of sin. I don't honestly believe that anybody who carries a load of guilt—heavy load of guilt—would say that we're making light of sin. Remember that you can't do anything bad enough to cause God to quit loving you. You ought to try forgiving yourself. If you cannot forgive yourself in the procedures that we've outlined, I suggest that you simply move out from yourself and put your hands on your own shoulders and say: "I forgive you."

Maybe in your mind you should just see Jesus coming and

picking you up in his arms, holding you tight, and saying, "I forgive you. You're still my child even though you disobeyed me, even though your home broke up, whatever. I still love you and you're still my child." Maybe you ought to practice saying, "God loves me. I've confessed my sins to God. I'm his child and he loves me." This does not solve the entire problem of guilt. You may have become entangled in devices you could not control. God did not intend for your life to be thrown on the ash heap of life, but he intends for you to have new life breathed into you and for you to be a new person. That's why we sing "Hallelujah!" That's why we sing songs of praise. The burden has been rolled away and the new Adam was made clean and pure in Jesus Christ. You can be clean and pure and new, too.

Stranded with Fear
Bill

*F*ear is no doubt the underlying problem of those with whom I counsel. I see people who are terribly afraid of life. They are so much afraid of life that they're almost afraid to move at all, and they spend most of their time trying to find out how they can hedge their bets so that life will not betray them. I encounter people who are not only afraid of living, but they are afraid of dying. Then I see some who are asking the ultimate questions about eternity. Some people are so afraid of living that they have set limits on life so narrow they cannot move. They're afraid to take any kind of risk, and they demand a guarantee that every venture they go into, even the venture of getting up in the morning, is going to be successful.

What are we afraid of? What are the things that really bother us? What are the things that push us to the point of distraction? A lot of people are like the one singing, "I'm tired of living and scared of dying" ("Old Man River"). In the last year of counseling, I have heard more people tell me about wanting to commit suicide than I have heard in the twenty years that I have been a pastor. Either they're getting more honest and open with me, or suicide is an ever-increasing obsession with many people. I am convinced that many people who have harmed themselves with drug and drink are doing it to commit a slow suicide, because they're trying to push something out of their lives.

I am neither a psychiatrist nor a psychologist, but I know that day after day I hear people tell me, "I'm afraid to live." As I tried to listen to the protests of the Sixties and some of the disillusionment of the early Seventies coming from our young people, I heard the same thing. I heard people admitting to me in effect: "I'm afraid to live in this kind of world." Not a week goes by that I don't hear people tell me they're afraid to live in a big city. People tell me they're afraid to live in the kind of economic conditions they're in. And I've had more than one person confess that they're becoming afraid to just go across the street to even get a salary check cashed because life seems to be so penetratingly devilish in this hour. Many people can't live because they don't have all the answers.

People who are technically and scientifically oriented are concerned that everything that happens has to have a reason. That's great. When it comes to building bridges, airplanes, roads, and buildings, that's the way it should be. Reliable engineers and scientists make our world a better place. The engineering mind has to anticipate every consequence. You have to know answers before an event. You must find ways to nail down everything that's going to make it go wrong. That's the way you're trained. Everything that happens has to have a reason.

There are others of us, however, who spend our time dealing with mystery. We try to get answers to unanswerable questions. We're the kind who have a dreadful time balancing the checkbook! Then the technically oriented come up against the mysteries of life and are frustrated because there are no systematic answers. Some people want a religious system where everything is answered. There are mysteries that God hasn't revealed to us. Even the time of his second coming was withheld from Jesus. I have a tremendously difficult time getting all people to learn to live with mystery. The Bible says: "Behold I show you," not a certainty but, "I show you a mystery."

Now I am not slapping the wrist of either kind of thinking, but I am saying that we somehow must learn to live with mystery. I don't know what tomorrow brings. I don't know what catastrophes may come across my life. I am not able to take every circumstance and control it. I am not able to control my fears, but Jesus said: "Fear not, I have been alive; I am alive now, but I was dead. Don't worry, I'm going to take care of your life." Do you see what that says? You don't have to nail down every circumstance. You don't have to cover every bet. You can't buy insurance for every situation. But you have to go through life knowing that ultimately God has his hand on you. And that's more important than anything else. Fear not. Don't be afraid to live.

I recently read an interesting article in *The New York Times* magazine section. Do you know that four times as many people are killed in their homes every year than are killed on the streets through violence? The article drew the conclusion that it's four times safer to be out on the street at night than it is to be in your home. Then the question was asked: But why is it that people don't want to be out on the street where they think they're going to be mugged? People can fall from a ladder or they can get into a family argument, violence erupts in the home, or an accident occurs and they're killed.

The answer given was this: In the home you feel you can control what's going on. You have some sense of management there, but out on the street you have no sense of being able to manage and you just have to trust. I don't know what that means except that we're going to have to live with mystery and understand that underneath are the everlasting arms of God. That's the only way we can make it. Not only are we not to be afraid of living, but God said: "Be not afraid; I will never leave thee nor forsake thee."

Not only should we have confidence in living, understanding that all men have been afraid at times—and Paul said, "Who is sufficient for these things?"—but we're going to have to be unafraid of dying. The Scriptures tell us that Jesus said: "I was dead and behold I am alive forevermore."

Death is the word least used in the American language. J. B. Priestly said that when he came to America, he enjoyed going to a dinner party and in the middle of the conversation injecting a conversation about death. He said that every time he did it, everybody immediately began to cut him off because they didn't want to talk about death. He said that Americans somehow seem to have created the idea that they will never die, and they will never have to face it. The cosmetic industries have tried to give us some defense against death and all of the jogging and vitamin taking are parts of our defense so that we'll never have to face it.

Jay Lipton of Yale University noted that the greatest unanswered questions in America have to do with death and the questions are still the same: Will we know one another in heaven? What will it be like for eternity? Yet men continue to die. Metterlock said: "I am a frightened child in the face of death."

Jesus said: "I have died." (I have already faced death.) Now let me remind you that if your Jesus is only a philosopher of the first century or if your Jesus is only a good man or only the best teacher that ever lived, it doesn't make much difference to you. But if your Jesus is the Son of God, born in the heart of God and delivered on this earth through the virgin Mary; if your Jesus lived among us as the sinless Savior of the world and was crucified, died, and went into hell to pay the price for all men's sins and is risen again, then you don't have to worry about death. For that's the Jesus that has overcome everything that we'll face; that's the Jesus who comes and takes us through those difficult hours.

The longer I live and the more I deal with people, the more I'm convinced of one thing: that the ultimate question of death cannot be answered in any other way. And those who have no religion may be able to make it in an academic debate somewhere, and those who have cut the supernatural out of their lives—pushed it aside and said they can live without it—have no answers for the ultimate. The only answer they can bring in is a big question mark. When a person has a question mark shoved in his face, life becomes tragic, for you cannot live with it.

John Wesley said: "Our people die well." When I read that on a page not too long ago, it jumped up at me and stabbed me. "Our people die well." Then I began to think of people I know who have faced death. I have stood by the beds of those who knew the Christ and who did not fear in their darkest hour. I will stand with John Wesley in saying that those who have walked with the Christ and into whose hearts the Christ has been born, die well, for they die unafraid.

Jesus said, "Not only am I alive but have been dead, and I have the keys of hell and death." Jesus speaks to the ultimate of our fears when he says not only don't be afraid of living and don't be afraid of dying, but don't be afraid of eternity. The Scripture quite clearly means he has the control of hell and death. Jesus said to his disciples: "Fear not; I go to prepare a place for you. If it were not so, I would have told you." This passage has been run by us so many times that it has grown smooth around the edges. Some of the best Greek scholars indicate that a clear interpretation of this passage would show that in the eternal world to come are special places prepared for God's people. I go to prepare a specific place for you. Jesus says that in the eternity I shall get it ready and I'm going on ahead. I go to get your room ready and I've taken care of eternity for you.

Death may be the ultimate fear of the human soul, but there are many times, when in the stress of living, the fact of dying is of little concern. We need help to cope with daily fears. Sometimes simply acknowledging the things we fear helps us to confront this "obstacle" head on. Fears are crippling and hinder our ability to live a wholesome, fulfilling life.

People are afraid to commit themselves to anything that will demand any performance. For example, marriage. I know any number of couples who are living together, thinking they can tell if they are suited to one another and thus avoid a costly divorce if it doesn't work out. Why should it work out? It's like rental property—you have nothing invested and somebody else takes care of the maintenance.

Some are also afraid to commit themselves to a church. They are afraid they may be asked to give of themselves or their resources (money, talent, time).

We're afraid of people. "They" may make fun of me. We may ask, "Do they like me or are they just trying to get me to do something for them?" Nobody wants to feel that they're being used.

Sometimes we never outgrow our childhood fears—darkness, storms, fear of being alone in an empty house, fear of the dentist or doctor or even teachers.

Both men and women face the fearful reality as they go to work each day that they must produce and please or lose their jobs.

Then there is that all encompassing, gripping, sick-at-the-stomach fear experienced by parents who see their teenagers grappling with situations which so easily could bring disaster or at least permanent scars to their young lives.

Is there an answer? People choose to cope with these anxieties in various ways. Sometimes our reaction to fear brings on more difficulty either to ourselves or for others—we never act without involving others. Some cope by taking tranquilizers or alcohol. Some people overwork to compensate. Sometimes fatigue and illness are the direct result of extreme anxiety. Sometimes a person beset with fears copes by committing suicide, because he fears death less than he fears life.

The only answer to fear is to take the words of Jesus—he spoke directly to the fears of mankind. He repeatedly says: "Do not be afraid, fear not." This was the explicit ministry of Jesus.

Farther back in the Bible, God continually spoke to the fears of his people. To Abraham he said, "I am thy shield and guarantee." To Isaac he said, "I am thy shield and buckler." To Jacob, when Joseph was lost down in Egypt, God said, "I will be with thee." When Moses and the children of Israel were at the Red Sea and Pharaoh's armies were coming onto their backs, God said: "Fear not, stand still and see the salvation of the Lord." Jesus, in his revelation to John on the Isle of Patmos, placed himself in the center of life and death when he said: "I am he that liveth, but was dead, and, behold I am alive forevermore."

A story I read not long ago shows how close eternity pushes in on the human heart. It was about a Confederate doctor during the Civil War who was riding over the battle-field after a very devastating battle, and he saw what appeared to be a dead Confederate soldier, his body mangled, in a grave. As he got off his mount to make sure whether life or death was present, he heard this semi-conscious soldier in the ditch saying in audible terms, "Here, here." The doctor knew there was life present and did all he could to bring the young man around. He gave first aid and through his skill was able to bring life back to the body.

Days later the doctor was visiting him in a hospital tent. He leaned over the bed of the young man and said: "While you were there on the battlefield virtually dead, the sign of life that I saw was that you kept uttering the words 'Here, here.' What was going on in your mind? Why did you utter the words 'Here, here'?" The young man said, "I remember it clearly, for at that moment I was lingering between life and death. I was already virtually on the other side. I could feel myself slipping out of this world and I heard them calling my name as though they were calling the roll over on the other side. I heard King Jesus call my name and all I could think to do was just to say, 'Here, here, I'm present.'"

We don't have to wait as the children of God until death comes to take us away to be present at the eternities—because eternity means now, and those of us who have given ourselves to Jesus Christ have the implantation of eternity in our hearts, and we live with eternity now. This means that we do not live bent over and beaten as men who have no hope, but we live as men who have the spark of eternity in their lives. This means that Jesus lives with us, not through some dead ethic but through a living relationship with us that shall give us a sense of the eternal.

A little girl returned from church where she had heard the preacher expound on the text: "And Enoch walked with God and God took him." The mother said: "Tell me about Enoch walking with God." The little girl smiled and said: "Well, Mother, I think it's something like this. Enoch and God went for a walk one day and it was a long walk. Toward the end of the day God turned to Enoch and said: 'Enoch, we've walked a long way today. I believe that it's closer to my house than it is to yours. Let's go on to my house now.'"

I believe with all my being that the believer needs to have no fear of life because Jesus is with him, of death because Jesus has already defeated it, or of eternity because Jesus is already there. And once you've settled the questions of life and death and eternity, you have settled all the questions of life. Jesus said: "Because I live, ye shall live too." Then the real opportunity is for us not to fear, for Jesus walks with us in life, in death, and for eternity.

Stranded in Illness
Carolyn

*T*wo of the most outstanding memories of my childhood concern close association with illness. I remember as a small child the Sunday ritual of Sunday School, church, dinner, and then always a ride to a community about eight miles from our home to visit Aunt Berta. To me she had always been old, but I'm sure she was only a little past middle age. She was a victim of crippling arthritis—confined to a chair all day. She always looked neat in a pink or blue dressing gown with a light blanket over her lap to cover her legs.

Aunt Berta was tortuously placed in that chair in a sitting room off her bedroom by early morning, and there she remained until late evening when the painful task of putting her to bed was accomplished. She was dependent on relatives and friends to take care of all her grooming needs and even to feed her. Her family had been part of the community for many years and the door of the big, old house was always unlocked for neighbors and friends to come and go. Aunt Berta was totally at the mercy of whoever chose to walk through that door.

Her house sounds like such a sad, drab place that no one would choose to visit her, but quite the opposite was true. It was a very happy place, always full of people—it was sort of the gathering place for the community with Aunt Berta the center of attention. She knew everything worth knowing and was a great story teller with a contagious chuckle. I remember that she eventually got so she couldn't even hold a fan (those were the days of fans, before air conditioning) to blow away a Florida gnat or fly from her face in the hot summertime. She made sure that no one left feeling depressed and sorry for her.

As I look back, Aunt Berta spent many years as a person condemned to one chair, one room. Her world consisted of what she could see from her window and the people who came to see her. Instead of being a sour, complaining, old cripple that we dreaded fulfilling a duty to visit, we always came away with some of the overflow of her sweet spirit. I think one of her greatest gifts to people was that she really listened to you. This is a gift that busy, active people don't always have. She listened to me, even a child. I was important to her, and it made me feel good.

One of the most heartbreaking and difficult situations to deal with is the prolonged, serious illness of a child. It is one matter to have the usual childhood diseases, but when a child is deprived of normal growing up activities over an extended period of time, it is a heavy load for the patient, the parents, and the other family members to carry.

We had an experience like this very close to our family. Before the days of vaccine for measles, there was the annual siege that went through my class in school. I was in the fourth grade and my best friend and I were quite sick. My friend's little brother was exposed and got sick with what was assumed to be the measles. It turned into severe strep throat and fever that remained an unusually long time. What started out to be merely a childhood disease turned into a nightmare of continual throat infections, strength-draining fevers, and near death. This once active little boy had to be confined to bed for almost three years.

Since I have a younger brother, also, I visited the family often and helped entertain him by reading and playing games with him. He never complained, and I'll never forget his sweet smile. His favorite activity was building model airplanes, and his burning ambition was to be a pilot. No one thought he would ever make it because of his weakened physical condition. Today he is a pilot for one of the largest airlines in the country.

His accomplishments are the result of how his family handled this confinement. To my knowledge, they never admitted defeat—surely they must have felt it both emotionally and financially at times. They were determined to do all they humanly could with God's help to allow this child to realize his dreams. Their determination was contagious and this, added to his overwhelming desire to fly, brought him through hard places.

The character, personality, and lifestyle of all closely involved with traumatic illness are likely to be altered in order to cope. I have seen the big, alert man at the controls in the cockpit of his huge airliner bringing it in for a safe landing. In my mind I remember the pale, thin face of a bedridden little boy as he worked over a model airplane. He was determined one of these days to be free from that bed and that room and to soar in spirit and reality above us all.

When Bill and I were married in August of 1953, we received many lovely gifts. Because my family had lived in Ocala, Florida, almost longer than anyone else, there were special meanings and love represented in the gifts. The first few years we were married many things had to be packed away for the time when we would have room for them. Bill had four more years of schooling, and a two- or three-room apartment gets to be a small place.

That summer Bill was the preacher on the Florida Baptist youth revival team. They had nine revivals scheduled with one week between the sixth and seventh. Bill drove to Ocala on Saturday after the sixth revival. We were married Sunday afternoon, and the following Saturday he returned me to my parents and went on with the team for the rest of the revivals. In the meantime, I had to move to a furnished garage apartment in Sanford, Florida, and start my teaching career. (Some men use any excuse to avoid moving chores!) The first thing I learned in that apartment was that we didn't need an alarm clock. Every morning the gentleman farmer who lived in the "big house" would get up before dawn, muster all his strength, and roll up the garage doors with a sound like misplaced thunder. Then just as my heart was calming, he cranked up his ancient Ford truck which shook the whole garage. I didn't mention this to Bill in advance. My revenge for being left for three weeks was the hysterical glee I enjoyed that first morning when all this noise took place, and Bill leaped out of bed thinking that the Lord had failed to warn him about the end of the world!

One of the first things Bill noticed in the kitchen was the prominent display of a lovely, colorful ceramic plaque of fruit. "I like that," he said, "but why of all the things we had to pack away, did you choose this to use?" Very briefly, I'll tell you what I told him.

When I was eight or nine years old, I had to go to a dermatologist in Jacksonville, and in his office waiting room there were many people with horrible skin problems and disfigurements. Child-like I tried to pretend that I wasn't there. It was sickening to see the deformities.

We had a long wait, and I noticed that my mother kept looking at a lady across the room, and finally their eyes met in recognition. They had been childhood friends in south Georgia. They hadn't seen each other since early teenage years. My mother introduced me, her daughter—and her friend introduced her daughter and I *had* to respond. This girl was about twelve or thirteen. As a small child she had fallen into an open fireplace, her clothes had caught on fire, and she had been burned almost to death. She had only nubs for arms, her chin and chest were one because of scar tissue, and she had many other problems. This woman was as proud of her daughter as my mother was of me. This girl was lovely in spirit and was going through painful surgery and therapy, attempting to adjust and be somewhat acceptable to the eyes of other people. Through the ensuing years the families exchanged news through Christmas cards. This pitiful looking girl finished high school and college and was teaching school. She had such a great personality that the children loved her and were devoted to being their best for her.

This lovely, hand-made plaque was her wedding gift to us, and I treasured it above all others. I can't imagine how she made it with no hands. Many days when I would come in from school tired and disgusted, it was hanging there as a symbol of superhuman effort and love. That plaque has hung in the kitchen wherever Bill and I have lived. It is now hanging in a place of special honor—in the kitchen of our cottage at Sky Valley. It represents many things to me—the sweet spirit, love of life, service to God and man of this girl who, because of an accident, has suffered immeasurably. I guess it is my challenge to quit my fretting over little things and get on with living.

Bill

When illness comes, there is a sense of having been separated from life—that life has passed me by and I'm caught here with this physical problem that will not let me develop as the kind of person I want to be. First of all, the people who are ill are separated in life. This sense of separation dominates them, and all of a sudden they begin to feel as though they're less than human.

I've been on the board of our Baptist Hospital. I think they do magnificent work and I have nothing but strong affirmation for it. I've noticed one thing in common about all hospitals. That is, if you don't watch it, the person who is in that hospital bed begins to feel as though nobody sees him as a human being. Patients are seen as a gall bladder, a heart attack, a liver ailment, or a broken arm. They're not human beings.

I was at the Veterans' Hospital several years ago visiting one of our members who had been a patient there for a long time. I walked into his room and we had a worthwhile visit. I was getting ready to leave and, to make conversation, I asked, "Are you getting good treatment?" It was a beautiful, brand new hospital—the corridors were filled with aides, nurses, and interns going up and down the hall being efficient. This patient looked up at me and said: "Pastor, I'm getting excellent care; there's only one thing wrong with it. I don't feel like a human being. I feel like a slab of meat on the bed that they come to stick pins in."

Now that has comic overtones except for those of you who have been ill. After awhile you're just hungry to have somebody call your name in a less than official capacity and really inquire of you: "How do you feel?" Not, what is your blood count? Not, what is your temperature? Not, what kind of liquids did you take in today? But simply, how do you feel?

I have never had a serious illness myself, but in 1967 I had what was for me a very serious illness—I had the mumps. Mumps is a low-sympathy disease. Now if I were to get sick again, I'd contract a high-sympathy disease, but that was my year for a low-sympathy disease. My two sons had the mumps, and I wanted to identify with them and so I got the mumps.

For years I'd been going to see people and holding their hands and praying with them very sympathetically, and I thought: Here's my time, now I'm going to get some sympathy. I did have some visitors. They would come and stand outside the window. Nobody would come in the house—they would yell in the window and then they would start laughing. Some of my doctor friends came and did that! They'd say things like: "When are you going to put away childish things?" This was funny for awhile, but soon the pain got very intense. My face and neck were so big that my beard rubbed a raw spot on my chest. This was the nearest I ever came to a sense of separation, because people felt as though somehow I would contaminate them, and I could have contaminated them. I began to feel with the mumps that I was an unclean person. My family would warn people: "Don't go back there; he's got the mumps. Have you had the mumps?" I felt very unclean.

Not only contagious diseases like the mumps, but things like heart attacks and cancer often give people the feeling that they're unclean. I grew up in a time and in a church where people never touched each other. And when I became a clergyman, I didn't touch anybody for a long time. I'd known some clergymen who had been accused of touching people the wrong way, at the wrong time, and had lost their jobs, and I certainly didn't want that. I'd go to the hospital to visit and see the patients there but *never touch them*.

Through a pastoral care program, I learned that I was reinforcing his feelings of being unclean by not touching the patient. Many ministers have learned to touch patients in a very delicate, loving way to let them know they're not unclean. Even though their bodies may have broken down, even though they're not able to be in the mainstream of life, we're here in the name of Jesus Christ to let them know that we love them and that they're not unclean.

You know, the New Testament depicts an interesting practice for those who were considered to be lepers—a vile disease, leprosy. They made the lepers hold bells out in front of them and ring the bells to warn: "I'm unclean; get out of the way." A lot of that, the scholars tell us, was not leprosy; it was just bad skin. They didn't have dermatologists in those days to get rid of those skin diseases, so anything that was a rash or looked terrible was considered to be leprosy. Those with the disease had to have the bells to ring all the time, indicating, "I'm unclean; get out of the way." Well, without realizing it, we do this to those who are ill. We reinforce the feeling of being unclean.

Those who are sick with very explicit diseases at least have something someone can see. When I had the mumps, you could see that I had the mumps. I want to mention our attitude toward mental illness (also see chapter 5). Now I know a lot of academic things about mental illness, and I've had enough training and been near it enough to have some personal feelings about it, but our culture still hasn't learned how to deal with people who are mentally ill. If the person with a heart attack or a gall bladder experience feels as though he is unclean, we intensify this ten thousand times for people who have mental illness. It's respectable to have a heart attack, but in our culture we have made it less than respectable to have an emotional problem. It's respectable to have a gall bladder problem, but we have made it a tragic matter to have a mental problem. We have come to the place where we let the body break down, but we will not let the spirit—the inner being, the mental, the psyche—break down, and we say by our attitudes to those with emotional or mental illness that they can't be that way because they're unclean.

I have a few suggestions here. I've heard people cry out that for years they went without help, draining the financial resources of their family, never wanting to be classified as one who needed psychiatric help—because once that brand was put on them, they felt they would never be able to live through it. They could remember the person in their community who had to have some mental help always being laughed at or ridiculed behind his back and they didn't want to be put into that category.

Do you know who breaks down the most? The strong, silent type who claim that they can bear and carry everything. And they bear and carry everything until they explode all over everybody, and then the people around them don't know what to do about it. I've noticed in my own counseling ministry that many will accept the help of a clergyman-counselor, but do you know that 47 percent of those who go to psychiatrists first go through clergymen to be referred, to make sure it's all right? I'm not trying to build up the office force of any psychiatrist. I am trying to tell you that if you have a strong sense of feeling that you need help or if, in the stillness of the night, you are wondering about your own particular balance, don't be afraid to reach out for help. Don't be afraid to find competent help.

You wouldn't be embarrassed to visit a doctor and tell him your heart feels funny. You wouldn't be embarrassed to tell him you have a skin rash. You wouldn't be embarrassed— and your friends around you would be supportive—if you broke your leg and needed an ambulance. Why should we be embarrassed if the mechanism of the internal being somehow gets out of step? It's nothing unclean to have that happen. What did Jesus do when he crossed the lake and went over to Gadara? He found the demoniac that the people had cast out and put in chains, but what did he do? He had pity and healed the man. The man came to Jesus, asked for help, and Jesus healed him.

What I want us to realize is that when people have something wrong with them, there is this barrier that comes down and causes them to feel separated from the world. And sometimes we reenforce the barrier. The community of faith and love does more work to bring healing than we can ever imagine.

Here you are with an incurable illness or with a physical handicap, or someone in your family is this way, or you suspect that you have it. (That's the worst thing the person who suspects that he has but won't go find out.) What do you do?

First, you've got to learn to accept yourself as you are. As a silly little illustration of this: I have always wanted to be six feet tall and to be a good athlete. I've always wanted to have a 28 waist and a full head of hair. The only thing I was able to do was to comb the hair differently. The rest of it is not the way I had idealized. One day I just took a good hard look at myself in the mirror and I said: "I'm going to accept you for what you are, five feet ten, a very bad athlete and one hundred eighty-five pounds of flab."

So now when I play golf, I'm not Jack Nicklaus; when I jog, it's the *Self shuffle*; growing hair has never been a talent for the men in my family and I'm not going to try to compete with anybody else. You just have to take yourself like you are.

Life passed you by—gave you a bad heart. It's not your fault you picked parents who had bad hearts. That's the way it is. You're going to have to take a good, hard look at yourself and learn that's the way you are. Don't judge yourself by a star athlete or by an all-American. You received a bad heart in the deal. Others with good hearts probably didn't get your brain and some other things you have. There are restrictions on their lives, too, and they have to accept that. That doesn't mean to give into it, that doesn't mean not to take care of yourself. You know how to live to be a hundred? Here's the *Bill Self Formula for Being a Hundred*: Get something wrong with yourself early in life and then "nurse" it; you'll watch yourself, you'll watch your blood pressure, you'll take your medicine, and you'll have great health except for this one thing. You'll be so concerned about this one thing that you'll watch your health every day and outlive the guy who has never had a sick day in his life!

I believe in divine healing. I strongly believe in God healing people, but I believe that God has chosen many instruments. One of the instruments that he has chosen is the medical profession. I advise you to get the best medical advice available. You should take all the medical resources that you have, bring them to God, and wait for God to let these resources take their proper place.

I want to tell you about a member of our church. She was an invalid who could only use her arms. I have no idea what was wrong with her. So many things were wrong with her physically. She had every kind of physical difficulty that a human being could suffer. Later, when circumstances changed, she was living in another part of the city, and I'd talk on the telephone about twice a week. You couldn't believe the physical difficulties she had. She was either flat on her back or standing up on crutches. To attend worship services she would stand at the back of the sanctuary on a pair of crutches because she couldn't sit down. She wrote a set of poems and a devotional book that were absolutely magnificent, and that illness squeezed out of her the finest spiritual insights that a person could have.

Just because your body isn't the body of an athlete, it doesn't mean that God has shriveled up your soul. I am reminded of Ralph, one of my church members in North Carolina. He had a crippling disease. He came to church in a little electric cart, and when we built the new sanctuary, we built a ramp so Ralph could ride his cart into the building. One stormy, snowy Sunday night as I got ready to go to church, I told my wife: "There won't be anybody there, but

I'm going to be there, and I'm going to preach a sermon, give an invitation, take an offering, and come home!" I traipsed through the snow about five blocks to the church. When I got there, the lights were on, and nobody was there but Ralph. All our people had cars with chains and snow tires except Ralph. He had come on that little electric cart. "Ralph," I said, "I told my wife we were going to have church." "Let's have it," he said. We didn't have a big offering, and he got tired of singing the invitation hymn, but we had a great service. I went home to get my car, took Ralph home, and later we returned the cart to him. It was an ordeal to get it worked out, and I let my congregation know it on Sunday morning.

Some time later one of the men in the church took Ralph and me fishing on the coast of North Carolina. We got to Ralph's house at four o'clock in the morning, and he'd been up two hours getting things ready. I went to the back door trying to be quiet. You don't ring the doorbell at 4:30 a.m. "Ralph, are you up? Are you there?" I heard a little rattle at the door, so I thought he must mean for me to come on in. I opened the door, walked in, and looked around for him. He was crouched over in the corner and flashed a light on an ape mask that he had pulled over his head and I tell you I've never been as frightened in my life as I was that morning. The driver of the car came in, revived me, and we got Ralph into the car, and he laughed all the way to the coast about that. There were ten children in Ralph's family, and seven of them had the same disease. Ralph looked at me and said: "God took my body away, but he didn't take away my spirit!"

Now that's what I'm talking about. I know a lot of you who have perfect bodies, a full head of hair, a good set of lungs, good brains, good education, and you're working at about 10 percent of what you ought to be doing. I know some of you who don't have much left. God has let your body go; you're fighting a disease; you're fighting trauma inside; the terminal date for you may be closer than it is for some of the rest of us, and you're going at 110 percent. Somehow in the economy of God, that's much more beautiful than those who are healthy and have everything, and are just plugging along complaining about life. The greatest Christian after the crucifixion and resurrection that ever lived was Paul. He was a rough, rugged individualist and we don't know what Paul's thorn in the flesh was. Some say he was blind or almost blind from the blinding light on the road to Damascus; others say he caught malaria the first trek across Turkey. (I believe that after having been to Turkey.) We don't know what it was, but we know that the word for thorn means a highly sharp object that pierces into your skin. Paul had been delivered from all kinds of crises. He had been in one miraculous event after another, but three times he went to the Lord and said: "Lord, take away this thorn in the flesh." Perhaps he was saying: "Lord, give me my sight back." "Lord, take away my malaria." Whatever it was, we don't know, but he said God told him, "My grace is sufficient for you."

Sometimes God is slow in his miracles, but when they are slow, he gives us a sense of his presence to get us through. How do you survive? I didn't say this is a cure. These are just a few things to get you through. Accept yourself as you are. Take the best medical advice available. Wait and see what God's going to do with you in the midst of it.

Dr. George W. Truett, the best preacher Southern Baptists have ever had, was suffering from a very severe illness. Dr. Truett could not sleep at night. I don't know why, but the illness did not give him a night's rest. One morning someone said to him: "Dr. Truett, aren't the nights terribly long?" He said: "No, they're not long enough. In the night when I cannot sleep, I spend my time praying for my people by name. The nights aren't long enough." That is the spirit that God gives us when we're trying to survive and we feel stranded by a difficult physical situation.

Stranded in Mental Illness
Carolyn

I became involved in a quarter of clinical pastoral education at Georgia Mental Health Institute through an
unusual series of circumstances. In many ways, this experience became a time of healing and of being accepted for
myself in a totally new environment. I entered the quarter
with the feeling of "sickness unto death" called despair. The
affirmation I received from patients, staff, peers, supervisor,
and my husband brought me a marvelous experience of
grace—of being acceptable and accepted. I especially want to
thank Mickie Griffin, a social worker with whom I feel a deep
bond of friendship, and Bill Emerson, my supervisor and
friend.

I believe that theology and mental illness cannot be separated. "What are people going to say about me?" is one of the
main questions patients begin to ask when they realize they
will soon be discharged.

John, the young, black, paranoid schizophrenic, describes
himself as feeling that his body is dead and only his spirit is
present. He is unacceptable to his family and community. He
has heard them call him a dog, and he feels that no one wants
him.

Jodi, a young wife and mother under terrific emotional
strain, would not allow her parents to be told that she was in
a mental hospital. She maintained that they wouldn't and
couldn't understand and would be humiliated.

Jim kept referring to an old woman he remembered from
his childhood who had been taunted by his community when
she returned from the state mental hospital. He feared this
reaction to him, even though he accepted the fact that times
and attitudes have changed.

Paul Tillich points out that grace is the *unity of life*. We cannot know the meaning of grace without first having experienced the separation of life. Grace is the reconciliation of the self with itself. A person has to be able to love himself before he can love others.

I have observed that as a general rule patients who require a long hospitalization are the ones who have the most self-contempt and hatred for others. They consider themselves to be very unacceptable. This is the place where despair finds entrance. Despair is the state of feeling separated from the meaning of life. When one feels meaninglessness and emptiness, despair (sin) abounds.

Tillich says, and I agree, that "despair is the sickness unto death." The Bible (Rom. 5:20) teaches that where sin (despair) abounds, grace much more abounds. "Grace strikes us when we are in great pain and restlessness. It strikes us when we walk through the dark valley of a meaningless and empty life. It strikes us when we feel that our separation is deeper than usual, because we have violated another life, a life which we loved, or from which we were estranged. It strikes us when our disgust for our own being, our indifference, our weakness, our hostility, and our lack of direction and composure have become intolerable to us." [1]

We simply have to accept the fact that we are accepted. Then we can experience the grace of being able to accept the life of another even if we do not like the things they do.

These case studies illustrate the many types of people who get stranded emotionally. These cases are typical of the stresses we all experience at some point in our lives. I chose these case studies to show that many circumstances—some of which we cannot possibly control—can bring us to the point of needing special help and care in experiencing the mental and emotional health of feeling accepted and acceptable.

A bad marriage, little or no education, poverty, over-indulgent parents, too much discipline, too little discipline, sorrow over rebellious children, drug or alcohol abuse, personal or family health problems, uncontrolled anger, and unreconciled guilt are only a few of the many causes of feeling separated from life. We need never be ashamed of seeking help from responsible professionals for ourselves or for family members. We have to risk exposing ourselves to those who can help and to realize that there are no apologies required.

John has haunted me since I've been at GMHI. His severe agitation that medicine couldn't seem to touch, the way he beat on the door and walls of the seclusion room and yelled for help, and seeing him put in a straight jacket really bothered me. I relived the time at Bryan's birth over fourteen years ago that I had a drug reaction and I thought I would be crazy the rest of my life. I stayed away from John until about a week ago when I started speaking to him and calling him by name whenever I saw him. On this morning when I spoke, he lingered and his answer to my greeting started the conversation.

C. How are you today, John?
J. Just livin,' that's all.
C. What do you mean, just living?
J. I'm just here, that's all. I'm a dead person, just my spirit is here. Do you believe that?
C. No, I don't. I'm talking to a real live person, not a spirit.
J. Do you know who I am? I'm the son of Muhammad Ali. That's who I am. Do you believe that?
C. No, I know that your name is John Smith. You know you are John because you answered when I spoke your name.
J. I don't want to be John Smith.
C. Why not?
J. Nobody likes me. They call me a dog. They say I'm no good. That woman took all I had. They really conned me. I don't know why she did that. I was good to her. I gave her all she wanted except a car. She just wiped me out. I'm scared of everybody.
C. Are you afraid of me?
J. No, but I'm scared of everybody. I'm scared of everybody

here.

C. Are you afraid of the patients and staff?

J. Yes. Everybody. They're just using me for a guinea pig here. Giving me so many medicines, and they took away my strength. They'll call me a sissy now.

C. John, they have to try different medicines to find the right one for you. When you get stabilized on the right medicine, you'll get rid of the bad reactions.

J. You think I'll get my strength back? I'm tired of this place and scared, but I don't have any place to go. Nobody wants me. I've been to heaven and hell. Did you know that?

C. No. You *felt* like you were in hell?

J. No, I was there—in hell.

C. What was it like?

J. I was there four days. It was dark and underground. They put me in a cage and I was in a cage alone in the dark.

C. You say "they" put you in a cage. Who is "they"?

J. The police. They locked me up.

C. Did you see anyone else there?

J. Yes. My dad. He was there.

C. What was he doing?

J. He was in a cage, too.

C. It is like being in hell to be locked up, I guess. You must feel pretty bad about that. You said you'd been in heaven, too. What was that like?

J. This place is heaven.

C. *This* place here?

J. Yes. Isn't this heaven?

C. Well, it's a nice place. We can feel like any place is heaven or hell, I guess.

J. How can I be saved?

C. What do you mean "saved"?

J. Will my soul go to hell and my body go to heaven?

C. No, I don't think so. I think your soul and body will go to the same place.

J. How can I keep from going to hell? I guess I'll just go to hell, and I don't want to.

C. Haven't you heard about being saved?

J. No, I don't know how. I guess I can't be saved.

C. It's very simple. All you have to do is to believe that Jesus, God's Son, died for your sins, and ask him to forgive you for your sins.

J. Is that all?

C. That's all. God made it very simple so that everybody could understand and believe.

J. But I'm so messed up. I've been going around here trying to save other people.

C. Nobody is too messed up for God to love.

J. You really think so? I know I shouldn't have run all those times. That just messed me up more. What do I have to do to get out of here?

C. I'm sure you've been told that many times, John. Keep on acting calm and sensible, and remember that you are John Smith. You can't be anybody else. You must prove to the staff that you can handle your situation without running away or doing something stupid.

J. You reckon I can?

C. Yes, I think so. You know, today is the first time you have let me talk to you. I like to talk to John Smith, and it's good to see you so much improved.

J. Really? You like me, OK?

(Another patient began to interrupt, and John started to move away but didn't want to be rude.)

C. Yes, John. We'll talk again.

This was the first time John had ever acted like he would talk to me. I always make a point of speaking to him by name and more and more he has responded, becoming more interested. I was surprised that he sat down and carried on such a lively conversation. In several instances, I made a point of letting him know that other people had feelings like he did and that seemed to interest him.

I picked up on some strong fears about his masculinity. Somehow in the conversation he said he didn't have any friends and mentioned that he should not have men friends. This related to his "loss of strength and being called sissy."

I am almost sure that John didn't need to be told about how to be saved. I wondered if he was just wanting to keep my interest. However, I got the feeling that he had been told he had better be good to get to heaven.

His description of hell is very appropriate for him since he has been confined to seclusion and restrained so much. I asked him if someone had told him this place was heaven and he was vague about that.

John has some very well-founded fears about his sexuality and even his identity. He also expressed in his way the feeling of being trapped, jailed by life. I have felt this trap myself and wonder how I could have better gotten this feeling across to John. He does need to feel like someone understands him.

Jim is a young man in his early thirties who came voluntarily to GMHI after attempting suicide with the exhaust of his car—the motor failed, but he was not found for about ten hours. He has not been working regularly for three months because of a virus infection and weather conditions. He has an attractive wife and two young children. His friends have rallied and have been very supportive since his suicide attempt.

Jim was standing on the porch enjoying the sun, and no one else was around. He greeted me pleasantly. He is in my group and has used the group therapy as well as any patient I've seen. Because of his sharing in the group, I know that he has deep feelings and that he has difficulty expressing them to his wife.

C. Jim, I've thought a lot about what you've said about not being able to communicate with your wife. I think I know how you feel. I've done my husband the same way you did your wife when you were upset and couldn't tell her about it.
J. I know she was upset. When she was bringing me back

up here, she said: "If I ask you something, promise you won't get mad." I told her that makes me mad when she says that. I don't like her way of doing that. But anyway, she asked me if I really loved her. She says if she knows I love her, then she can go through anything. I don't know why she asks that. She's been doing that since I've been here—she never did before. It's like she thinks she's responsible for me being here.

C. That's a heavy load for her to carry.

J. Yeah, it really is. I guess it is partly because we haven't understood each other. I'd try to talk to her and she'd say not to worry, that everything would be all right. That makes me mad. Then I'd been working twenty hours a day—brought home a check for $200, and she threw a pile of bills in my lap that added up to $400, and I just couldn't face it. I thought, *What's the use?* and started figuring out a way to kill myself.

C. It's awful to feel that bad. I was so worried one time that I tried to figure out a way to run away, but I couldn't see a way to escape.

J. Well, I almost did it, but it wasn't my time to die, I guess, because if the car hadn't shut off, I'd have been gone. I'm glad now I didn't die. I want to live. I hate to think what would have happened to my kids if I had killed myself. What I live and work for are my two children and my wife. You know, it's a funny thing. I've been able to tell you and Mickie things that I've never been able to tell my wife. She's coming this afternoon to talk, and I'm nervous about it. It's like meeting a stranger.

C. She's probably pretty nervous about it, too.

J. Why do you think she tells me she loves me and then says that if I don't want to come home, it's OK if that's what is best for me? I want to go home; but I'm scared, and I don't know why.

C. I can't answer for your wife—you should ask her about it. My guess is that she's trying to let you know that she loves you so much that she'll do whatever is necessary for your happiness. She probably associates your uneasiness when you were there last weekend with your suicide attempt. You said that when she asked you what was wrong you said, "Nothing." I found out lately that I've really been upsetting my husband by doing that same thing to him. I'm trying to change that.

J. If I told her, she wouldn't really listen. She'd just tell me everything will be all right and that makes me mad. She'll say: "If I tell you something, promise you won't get mad." _____, I'm mad already then. If I say, "Yes, I'll be mad," she just clams up and won't say anything else.

C. Sounds like you're playing a game that a lot of people play. It ends up with a lot of hurt feelings and communicating only anger. I think when a person has grown up not expressing any feelings, it is hard to ever really open up with anyone—even a husband or wife. I found out that my husband really wants to know what's going on with me. Sometimes even when I'm not sure what's bugging me, it helps just to acknowledge that and not just say, "Nothing," and clam up.

J. That makes sense, but it sure would be hard to do after all these years. Even my friends have cussed me out for not telling them I was worried and depressed.

C. Maybe we expect people to read our minds and feelings. That's putting all the responsibility on them, don't you think?

J. I never thought of it that way, but it makes sense.

C. I think that's why Mickie is so anxious for you to go to the mental health clinic after you leave for follow up. It will help both you and your wife to learn and remember to be open with each other.

Jim reminded me of my own difficulty in communicating. I saw in each spouse the hurt that comes when either feels shut out by the other. We also talked about the fact that everybody has problems and that we don't have to be ashamed and embarrassed but we often are.

I see in Jim a strong, silent, independent man who is now

troubled by his feeling of dependence on Mickie and GMHI. He says he was a walking dead man when he came here and that Mickie and others have "brought him back to life." I guess this is like him not wanting to leave the womb again.

Betty is a young woman who came to GMHI on a judicial commitment. Her two children had been taken from her and placed in a foster home. Her record mentions paranoid delusional thoughts and possible acute schizophrenia. Her medical examination revealed possible cancer of the cervix.

Betty was the first patient I was exposed to at GMHI. She is in my group, so I have been with her every day at group time. I ran into her frequently, and we always exchanged a few pleasant sentences. One of the main problems of the staff concerning the patient is her refusal of treatment for the possible cancer. I really felt I should try to encourage her to take care of this matter.

Wednesday evening I asked Betty to walk with me up to the office while I checked in as chaplain on duty. I knew she was nervous about going to the hospital for treatment at nine o'clock Thursday morning. Her therapist had asked me to talk to Betty if possible. She had been very angry and accusative to her therapist and the doctor.

We talked about various things as we walked. We came back around by all the cottages, and she waited while I went into the cottages and checked with the staff.

When we were almost back, I tried to focus in.

C. Betty, are you anxious about going to the hospital tomorrow?
B. No, I'm not worried, really. I am concerned about the way I'm being treated. They're just giving me the run around. I just want to be sure they don't do a hysterectomy or tie my tubes.
C. They aren't going to do that, Betty. The therapist and doctor have talked to you about that and told you how important this treatment is, haven't they?
B. Yes, but I don't see why I can't get it done by my own

doctor. I don't trust anybody here. My husband has influenced them into doing something to me.

C. How can that be?

B. He has ways. I know him. He wants to keep the children away from me. And all I want is my children. I don't see why I have to have this treatment here. I can do it when I get out and have my own doctor.

C. I think they are afraid that something might come up to keep you from seeing your doctor right away. You don't seem to understand the urgency. Your Pap test came back showing a malignancy—cancer—this is serious, Betty.

B. How do I know that is true? I don't trust anybody here. When I came in, the doctor said I had an infection, and I thought they'd just give me some medicine. I had a kidney infection before, and the medicine cleared it right up.

C. This isn't like a kidney infection. This is on the cervix and seems to be in the early stages.

B. They didn't tell me it was cancer. (She started crying.)

C. I thought surely you heard them say the report showed a malignancy.

B. Well, I didn't, and I'm not at all sure they're telling the truth. I want another doctor's opinion. Have you seen the lab report?

C. Yes, I saw it attached to your record, so I know they are telling the truth. Doctors and hospital staff don't allow themselves to be influenced by outside pressures. I'm sure they'll arrange for you to have another doctor's opinion on this.

B. I really don't care what they do to me if I could just be with my children. (Sobbing.)

C. Let's sit down here till you feel better. Betty, I really want you to know that the staff is telling you the truth. Probably the sooner you get the medical problem taken care of, the sooner something can be worked out about your children. I don't know all that's involved, but I do know that they care about you and want to do what is right.

B. I just feel like it's no use. I just sit here day after day and wonder about my kids and what they must think of me. I don't care if I do have cancer. If I can't have my kids, I'd rather die anyway. (Cries more and more.)

C. Betty, I'm so sorry. I know that doesn't help the situation, but I do care about you.

B. Well, you're the only one I can trust around here. (Long minutes pass.)

C. Would you like for me to pray for us? (She nods yes. I hold her hand and ask God to help Betty in all the ways she needs help—health, children, job and all—and to give her added grace and strength for the days ahead.)

B. Thank you, Carolyn. I'll go in now.

C. I'll stop by before I leave tonight, Betty.

My relationship with the patient has grown since I first came to GMHI, and I am really fond of her. I have a sinking feeling that she has really been given a raw deal concerning her children, and it will take forever if it ever is straightened out. Her therapist has asked me to get Betty to acknowledge the fact of cancer. They had not gotten through to her. So I really had a purpose in directing the conversation. The nurses saw her crying as a real breakthrough, because she had been so unemotional about everything.

If crying is what she needed, we really got results because she has cried since then, also. She has also agreed to have the necessary surgery after having another doctor's opinion.

I felt comfortable in praying for Betty because I knew she is religious and it was the only comfort I could offer her, other than my presence and feeling with her. I felt ambivalent about this interview because of the obvious emotion expressed. I want to *do* something for her, and it is hard for me to acknowledge that I can only *be with* her.

I have had a number of conversations with Bob. He planted the flower seeds I brought, and we played checkers last Wednesday evening. He is a very meek person and always seems pleased to pass the time of day with me. He had told me last Friday that he was going home for the weekend and planned to buy a trailer. Today (Monday) as I was leaving to go home, he stopped me at the water fountain and said: "I got the trailer." I had to think fast to get the significance.

B. I got my trailer this weekend.
C. That's great, Bob. Tell me about it. (We sat down, and he was drinking coffee.)
B. I got the key right here in my pocket. It's on the way to where I work.
C. Is it in a trailer park or in somebody's yard?
B. It's in a friend's yard, and it's real close to where I work. They really want me to come back to work. They really need me.
C. I'm sure they do. Did you talk to your boss about your job?
B. Yes. He says he sure needs me. I do body work on trucks. I put the body together on those great big old trucks. I do good work real fast.
C. Good workers like you are hard to find. Did you see your family?
B. Yep. They came up there to see me. Did you know me and my wife is [sic] divorced?
C. No, you hadn't told me that. Does she have the children?
B. The judge gave me the two boys and her the girl. I hadn't seen my little girl for such a long time, and she was so glad to see me. She liked my mustache. My wife is wanting to come back to me. She says: "I want to get back with Bob, and I won't be satisfied till I do." But she'll do the same thing again—run around on me. Do you know when my boys was [sic] babies, I'd come home from work, and she wouldn't have nothing for us to eat, and I'd have to wash diapers and hang them up to dry. I'd wash diapers till midnight so the baby could have clean diapers. And every time I'd get the house fixed up, she'd tear it to pieces. Last time she left I told her that was it. Did I ever show you my boys' pictures?

C. No, but I'd like to see them.
B. Wait right here and watch my coffee and I'll go get them.
C. They're really good looking boys. What are their names?
B. This one's Bobby and here's Buddy. Would you believe they were both premature?
C. They certainly look healthy now.
B. Yes. I don't know about my wife. She used to be a pretty girl. We used to get along real good. You know how we met? On the church bus—she saw me and wrote me a note to meet her at church, and I did and then I gave her a ring—you know the first one you get—kept the other till we got married. Yep—we used to get along fine—me and her—me and her. (Those words were spoken wistfully and with watery eyes.) I don't know why I can tell you all of this. You understand me.

During the conversation somewhere, Bob told me that he cannot read or write and how he used to keep his head lowered on his desk to avoid being questioned by the teacher. I am upset with a teacher who didn't pick this up and take the trouble to teach him basic reading and writing. Part of his illness is lack of ability to cope with life. A little education would have helped.

He also indicated that what he really wanted was to be able to work and come home to a good meal and someone to care for him. When you think about it, that honestly isn't much for a person to want out of life, but even that seems to be an impossible goal for some people. Someone to care for Bob would solve at least part of his problems and help him cope. No one can live isolated from the warmth of other people. It is like warming cold hands over an open fire when human beings extend warmth to each other.

Linda is a lovely young girl in her late teens who was admitted to the hospital in a schizophrenic episode after having seen the movie *The Exorcist*. She also had other problems concerning family and boyfriends.

This interview is mainly one of feeling. As we walked out the door, the fresh cool air hit us sharply, and we both took a deep breath.

L. Feels good out here.
C. It surely does.
(We walked slowly toward the front by way of several cottages and across the grass to the front walk.)
L. Is it OK if I smoke?
C. If you want to. How are you feeling today?
L. Better now. I had a headache this morning, but it's better now. It feels good out here.
C. Yes, and look at the beautiful dogwood trees.
L. I love flowers.
(We walked to the dogwood trees and she looked closely at the blossoms—almost studying them. Then she saw the pink and white azaleas, caught her breath, ran over to them, fondled the blossoms and smelled them.)
L. I can't smell them but they're so beautiful. They feel so tender.
C. They are tender and lovely. I am enjoying being with you.
L. Me too.
(We walked down the sidewalk by the azaleas, dogwood and daffodils, and we lingered as she seemed to be seeing them almost for the first time.)
L. Sometimes I like to walk up to the street and watch the cars go by.
C. Well, let's walk up that way. Did you talk to Mickie today?
L. Yes, and she's going to see if I can visit my mother this weekend. I hope I can.
C. I hope so, too. I'm sure your mother will do her best to work it out.
(We watched the cars go by, and I could feel her getting tense.)
C. Let's walk back down toward the back. Look here along the fence at the beautiful violets. I'm so glad to see the violets. When I was a little girl, we always went to the woods in very early spring to look for violets.

L. I like the woods.
(We stopped and spoke to three huge German Shepherd dogs through the fence. I started to caution her not to get too close when they started barking, and we moved on. We made our way down the hill at the back of the property, examining rocks and bugs and other interesting things along the way. We came to the playground and the jungle gym was inviting to me.)
C. I wish I had on slacks so I could climb.
(Linda gave me a funny look.)
L. Do you think I could climb?
C. Sure—go head.
(She climbed to the top and grinned down at me proudly.)
C. Aren't you something!
(She got stuck coming down—had to have a little help. She walked over to the merry-go-round and ran her hand over the rail.)
C. Get on—I'll give you a spin.
(We laughed as she staggered when she got off and started down the hill. We stopped and watched some boys playing basketball. As we got near the cottage:)
L. That was fun. I like to have fun.
C. I do, too. It was fun for me.
(When we got inside, I walked down the hall toward her room with her.)
C. Linda, it's time for me to go home now. I'll be back about noon tomorrow. I hope you'll have a good evening.
(Linda turned to me, hesitated, and simultaneously we hugged each other.)

Emotional or mental illness can occur in any family and should be treated like any other illness. As life becomes more complex, we must acknowledge the need for help and understanding.

[1] Paul Tillich, *The Shaking of the Foundations* (New York: Charles Scribner's Sons, 1948), p. 161.

Stranded Alone
Bill

*T*he other morning as I was going to the television station, I began to be aware of all the people standing at the bus stops. Many of you may ride the bus to work. I encourage you to do it. That means you can get out of the way so I can drive my car on to wherever I'm going, and I'm all for that.

I have observed that there must be something about standing at a bus stop that is a dehumanizing experience because there seems to be a glassy-eyed stare in everybody's eyes. I guess in the five hundred bus stops I've passed in all of my vast experience of passing bus stops, I have only seen one time when the people waiting there were talking to each other. I was making my usual bus stop poll the other day as I drove along Peachtree Street, and at one of the bus stops, there were about ten people all laughing and talking, and I thought: You can't do that; you won't fit into my sermon Sunday night!

Have you ever wondered what the thirty-year-old secretary feels like as she realizes that she may be alone for the rest of her life?

Have you ever wondered what the thirty-five-year-old accountant feels like in his little bit out-of-date Brooks Brothers suit standing there with *The Wall Street Journal* tucked under his arm, knowing that for the rest of his life he may be going back and forth on that bus route to the same job and be alone?

Have you thought about the young person with books under his arm about to face the onslaught of students and professors who may prove him stupid?

Have you ever wondered what the widow feels like when

she has to get up every morning and face a cold house and memories that are beginning to become a little bit faded?

Have you ever wondered what happens in the life of a person when he finally wakes up one morning and faces himself squarely and begins to confess that life has passed him by?

Have you ever been aware of the kind of pain that is experienced by one who has seen a marriage—that started with all the glory that a marriage could have—suddenly begin to crumble? They couldn't stop it, and it turned to dust in their hands because of things that were out of their control, and then they wondered what they were going to do with life.

For the widow or the widower or the divorcee to begin to come back into the mainstream of life is a very difficult thing and, frankly, I don't believe the singles bars or the singles apartments really provide the kind of community they're hungry for. I don't actually think the church does a good job of community, although I think our church is working at it and, hopefully, the day will come when we will be better equipped to do the kind of work we want done in this area.

On television recently, I used the story of a thirteen-year-old boy who was lost up at Rabun Bald near Clayton, Georgia. Those are wild mountains up there. He was with the Sierra Club, and they were hiking in the woods and for some reason he wandered away. When he wandered away, he was thirty-six hours away from help, stranded in those mountains.

If I correctly remember the account in *The Atlanta Journal-Constitution* magazine section, he did not have a knife with him but had a few other things. He had to make a decision about what to do, and he used all the resources he had, all the wits about him. In a heroic attempt, he found his way out of there and back to people.

After I had shared that on television, his mother called me. I didn't realize it was his mother when the call came. I returned the call and she said: "I'm the mother of the young man you talked about on television this morning." And I got deathly ill right here. I thought: *What did I say? I hope it was good.* We chatted awhile, and she was pleased with what I had to say.

She said: "Tell me exactly what you said." She was a pleasant lady, and she had good insight into the situation and related something that I am at liberty to repeat. She told me that there was a point in the boy's experience where, in his own mind, he had to make a decision—a decision whether to give up and let the elements have him or whether he was going to pull his courage together, pull together all he had, and get out of those woods. He had to decide that he was going to live. Rabun County and the wilds of north Georgia were not going to swallow him up. "I'm going to get out of these woods and I'm going to take what I have—a tarpaulin, a few trinkets for the woods, a few things to hang onto, and I'm coming out of here."

Now that's the sort of attitude I want you to have. I don't know what your circumstance may be. You may be a widow in that apartment; you may be a thirty-year-old woman with a few flecks of gray in her hair. I don't know what it is, but I hope you can have a spirit which will cause you to pull yourself up and determine that you're going to leave those woods you're in. This is a survival kit, and if life's left you alone, this is for you.

First of all, there are twelve and a half million people in America who live alone. I guess of all I hear and see all day long the idea of loneliness is the feeling that seems to dominate. It's the thing that runs through the inmost self of people.

There are many couples who are lonely. Just because you're married doesn't mean that you don't have loneliness gnawing at the fringes and edges of your life. It may not be right up in front of you, you may not have the physical evidence of it, but it's there nonetheless.

I know some older people who are alone, too. It isn't the disease of the young. There's nothing more lonely than being sixty-five or seventy years old with the feeling that life has put you out on a shelf. Our society is dehumanizing to older people. The only rebellious organization that I agree with is the Gray Panthers—older people who are determined that they're going to lick this society's concept of age. Right on! I think we should have sent them to Vietnam! They'd have cleaned it up earlier because there's nothing stronger than a gray-haired-grandmother type with righteous indignation in her eyes and an umbrella in her hand. She'll clean up anything. There's a lot of strength and wisdom and ability. For those of you who are young, don't think the old don't have it.

Two years ago we traveled in Israel, one hundred and eleven of us. Those of us who were young became tired, but those who were old kept right on going. One whose age I don't even know (and she won't admit it) out-walked us all and then simply smiled and asked, "Can't you all keep up?"

Loneliness is a common disease. There's a poem I found that suggests:

> Yes, in the sea of life enisled
> With echoing straits between us thrown
> Dotting the shoreless watery wild
> We mortal missions live alone.

And then another poem, by Longfellow, suggests:

> Ships that pass in the night . . .
> Only a look and a voice; then darkness again, and a silence.

Whether you're a child and it's your first day at school, a preacher in a large church, the president of a company, the president of the nation, or one who hasn't made it up from the bottom, the feeling of aloneness is always there. T. M. Ling, the psychiatrist, observed: "Loneliness is the major social evil of our day." One psychiatrist did a study and found that in four hundred and nine suicides, one hundred twelve or 25 percent of them lived alone. It is a common disease in society.

Florence Nightingale was very lonely, so the records state; and she was lonely because her ideas were unusual and made her feel as though she were separated from her family. City dwellers feel that they have cornered the market on loneliness. When traveling on country roads in any section of the nation, I have observed people of all ages sitting on their porches watching the cars go by. Sometimes you see a family reunion going on and a warm feeling spreads out and envelops even the passenger in a passing car. That's a good feeling.

You also get a warm feeling when you see a farm house with smoke curling from the chimney and you know that the man stooped over carrying the buckets will be going in soon to a good meal and warm place by the fire. The very next farm house you pass may have a red-haired, freckled-faced boy hanging restlessly on the gate, staring at you as you go by as if to say: "Stop, take me with you; I'm bored and sick of this place." Or you may see a run-down house with sagging porch and torn screen door where you see a tired-looking woman with stringy hair and a flock of children running like chickens loose in the yard—the woman straightens up and pauses in her hoeing the turnip patch to watch as you drive by—longing, for what?

Walk down the street of any size town and you find the same mixture of people. Some towns are very clannish and consider all newcomers to be intruders. If you weren't born there, you don't deserve to live there. This feeling spreads to church, school, and throughout the community. So moving to a small town might not solve the loneliness problem.

Perhaps parents sometimes feel deserted by their children as they see them leave home, being moved around by corporations; then that awful feeling as they see their friends in illness and death—they started out with a full house and large circle of friends, and they are deserted at the end. You can be just as lonely in a cozy house in a small town or rural setting as you can in a cold steel and concrete apartment high rise in a big city.

The city seems to be the collecting place for a multitude of people who feel stranded. Most of the people I deal with—and of course in a counseling situation it would be the case—are those who feel that for one reason or another life has passed them by. They have been abandoned by life or betrayed by life, and they are left with the bits and pieces of it and somehow they feel God has abandoned them.

That's the reason I become upset when an athlete or a beauty queen is brought before a group as a great success symbol. They tell all the success side and on the other side all those who aren't either beautiful or athletic begin to wonder what's wrong with them. I've had that problem every time I've heard either one of those "success" testimonies. I prayed and God never did give me a contract with the Jets. You see the point. But most of us in life are not superlatives and merely get along with what we have, wondering why life didn't give us more. We're one-talent guys who just plug along.

Many times in the church we have a habit of playing games. There are ways of playing games where all of us are successful. You have a problem? You're unclean if you have a problem. We make nonsuccessful people feel out of place, because there's something wrong with them. It makes me awfully angry when we do this to people.

I have seen people who have either lost their jobs, gotten into trouble, had moral calamity whatever it may be, all of a sudden feel as though they couldn't come to church because they were unacceptable. I've seen this happen particularly with men when they've lost their jobs or have been demoted. They somehow felt as though they were not worthy to come to church. And we've done this with divorced people; we've done this with moral outcasts. If I read the New Testament correctly, Jesus spent considerable time with those who were on the fringes of society, with the broken people. In fact, God's great disinherited come in for the bulk of Jesus' attention.

Then as I looked at the city, I determined that not only

was it the collecting place for people who were alone, but I determined also that the city seemed to be giving nothing to these people. Every institution in the city that I observed seemed to be a dehumanizing institution. The schools are gone, the civic clubs in many cases are having trouble, some of the churches are in trouble, but the church is the only place where you can meet on a common ground and people can, theologically anyway, accept you for what you are as a human being with needs.

As all of this came together in my mind, I decided to call this a *Survival Kit for the Stranded*, a kit for those who feel like life has passed them by and left them stranded. I'm not going to give any answers for how to make it. I'm not going to take any wall flowers and make bouquets out of them.

But I hope by the grace of God I can give courage and let you know that you're a human being in the eyes of God. God hasn't abandoned you; God still loves you; and the church of the Lord Jesus Christ loves you.

But the fact that impressed me, as I studied this, was that Jesus himself often felt alone. There was nobody in the Bible, and consequently nobody in the world, more lonely than Jesus was on Good Friday when all of his friends had deserted him and the soldiers nailed him to a cross, and he cried out: "My God, my God, why have you forsaken me?" And if you would be honest with yourself and with me, there have been times when in the shallowness of that apartment, in the emptiness of wherever it is you are, in the anonymity of that office, and in that deadening experience of being jostled around in the crowds of the city, you've cried out of the gut, out of your heart: "My God, why?" It's there. Your rage at being deserted and passed over by life is there, and my rage for you is there.

Mark relates that the disciples went with Jesus "that they might be with him" because they recognized apparently that he was lonely. Now may I hasten to say that there's a difference between loneliness and solitude. Solitude is what all of us want at times—we're alone but aware that God cares. Jesus loved his solitude, and the one thing that I crave the most is solitude so I can get the batteries charged.

But when you're lonely, it's different. You're alone and you're out of contact with your life's support systems. I want to stop here and put down a peg. All of us have life-support systems. I became aware of that expression when I was reading about the astronauts going into the sky, and they talked about their life-support systems, whatever they were—the electricity in the ship, the rocket fuel to get them back, the food in the ship, the oxygen—they kept a constant reading on their life-support systems.

One day I had a call from a man who wanted to talk to me about moving to his community and working as president of his institution. It wasn't in God's plan; it wasn't for me; it wasn't the thing to do, but I enjoyed the glamor of being asked. He said: "Oh, Bill, why won't you do it? Don't give me the pious talk; come on and tell me."

I replied: "Well, the pious talk means something to me, but I'll be real straight with you. I believe that to do that would take me away from my life-support systems because I draw strength out of my congregation, and I could not live without them. They feed me as much as I feed them—sometimes more—and all of my life systems are intact, and I cannot move away from them." And the more I thought about that, the more I was impressed with the fact that many people cut themselves off from their life-support systems. You cut yourself off from people and then say, "Nobody likes me." We cut ourselves off from friends and then say, "Nobody feels friendly any longer." We begin to pull down shades and barriers; we begin to withdraw more into ourselves, and we somehow find reasons to justify being there. Then in this kind of walled existence we begin to cry out: "It's cold in here." We find we've trapped ourselves.

There are some life-support systems I think everyone must have. I think you need to have a life-support system of a work: some kind of work that will get you out of where you are. I don't know whether you're a "my wife will stay at home and be a submissive wife" type or whether you're a "my wife's gonna go out and work" type. But whatever type you are, everybody, including your wife, needs a life-support system; needs something that makes her or him feel as though they're worthwhile. Work is not a curse. Work is a blessing and a privilege.

It may sound like a Puritan ethic, but I have seen very few people who didn't work who were happy about it. We even keep statistics on the unemployed because that's considered dangerous in our culture. You need people. Now your work people cannot become your primary *people* people (that sounds funny, but you know what I mean). You can't make the people you work with your family. They can become your secondary family, but they cannot become your primary family. You can receive some strength and sustenance from them, but if that family thing becomes too much, what's going to happen when that virtually becomes your family and then some of them get transferred?

I was at a department store the other day and while I was there, the clerk who was waiting on me said: "You know, I've been here for X years, and it's not the same any more. We used to be a family here in my department and then they changed things all around and changed management and I'm left here. Nobody else is here that used to be here. It's not a family any more." I said: "Where do you live?" She told me she lived alone, had been a widow for many years, and the children were gone. The primary family had been her department and when they began to change it, her primary family fell apart.

You need people around you. You need work people and you also need people that you're involved with. I don't know who they are going to be. You will have to determine who they are. It may be a substitute family like the career group in your church, a missionary circle, a Sunday School class, a book club, or some kind of substitute family like that. It may be a good friend for whom you can become an aunt or uncle. It may be that you can in some way get involved with someone else that will keep you out of your shell. It may be somebody else about whose problems you can worry. You need that second kind of people for a life-support system.

You need something worthwhile to do for somebody else. I don't know what I would do if I were alone. Granted that I'm talking from secondary experience. I have had fits of loneliness, but it's a different kind. I think you need to do something even if it's some kind of busy, volunteer work.

I went to our Scoup (Single Career Obviously Unattached People) group one Sunday night after church, and I thanked them, when I finally got up to speak, for letting me in between the announcements! Out of a forty or fifty minute meeting, the first thirty minutes are announcements about things to do. You have to be healthy to be in that group! I listened to those announcements and I was tired. All of a sudden it occurred to me. They're being involved with each other; they're being involved with other people. That is the life-support system for them. I complimented them on having enough of whatever it takes to get it all together.

I have a sneaking suspicion that what I'm saying is not getting to the heart of the problem. But I also have a strong suspicion that the kernel of this sense of loneliness can only be dealt with by you. As you walk around the parameters of it and touch certain chords in it, you can begin to respond. Hopefully, I'm digging up the dirt at the bottom and letting it sift down again, and maybe it will come down another way. There was a lady who came to her pastor and complained: "I can't do anything for anybody; nobody loves me anymore." Her pastor answered her: "People love those who are lovable. Get involved with them, and you'll love them, and they'll love you."

Naturally, I think the church has a vital part in this because we're not out to take anything away from you. Don't be like the lady who spent $35,000 for dance lessons in this city because she was lonely, and they paid some attention to her. (The case is now in court.) Or don't be like the lady in Florida I read about recently. Her friends saw her in a wheelchair at the shopping center and they said: "What are you doing in a wheelchair?" She said: "Well, I found out that nobody pays any attention to an old lady walking around in a shopping center, but if I'm in a wheelchair, everybody helps." There will be a run on wheelchairs tomorrow!

If my antennae are correct, those of you who live alone have a sense that everybody has deserted you; that the church has geared itself for family groups. That may be the case, but I think some churches have recognized the need of a ministry to those who are alone.

Then remember that God wants to end man's loneliness. God actually does want to end man's loneliness. The whole Bible, read from this perspective, is to be God's avenue of getting to man to end his aloneness, because the root of aloneness is separation and the root of separation is sin.

I am not saying that because you're alone, you're sinful, but I am saying that you can have a family of twenty-five people around you and still feel lonely if there are things in your life that have put separation between you and others and you and God.

Remember that Jesus himself had these lonely periods. His family thought he was mad, and they deserted him. His friends deserted him in the garden. They could not face his trial, and they ran at the crucifixion. But recall that God said to Joshua: "As I was with Moses, so I am with you." And we have the promise in the New Testament: "Lo, I am with you always." And earlier in the Psalms: "Yea, though I walk through the valley of the shadow of death, I will fear no evil for thou art with me."

There are many times when people have no one to lean on, seemingly no one who cares—and that is when what we are deep inside counts the most. When you are rolled down the hall to the operating room, or when you are the one waiting for word concerning a loved one; when you wake up in the wee hours of the morning alone and afraid of the night noises; when death has left you desolate; when you pace the floor, moaning to God about your teenager—these are some of the times when only a strong, tested faith in God can see you through. God does love us, and he does care about each individual and his personal pain. Don't hesitate to cry to God, in Jesus' name, to help you bear your pain. Talk to him freely about the things that you worry about—isn't that what you want with *your* child? God is our Father and can both comfort us in times of trouble and rejoice with us in happy times.

Don't forget your life-support systems: people and family, work and projects. My last thought here comes out of a paper written by a young man who built giant walls between him and everyone else. In this paper to be shared with a group he said that he was angry with them because they didn't break down the wall, come in, and drag him out. The group responded with: "We couldn't get in there; you kept us out."

I say to you: Don't build the walls so big and so heavy that you can't get out, and don't be angry with people or churches or institutions that don't come crashing in to tear the wall down. I think maybe we ought to have a wall-breaking-down ceremony—a way in which we all crawl out of ourselves and we confess: "Here I am; I don't have anything to hide; I'm not successful; I'm not pretty; I'm broken; I hurt; I cry; I've got pain; I've been divorced; I'm widowed; I have a bad marriage or crazy kids or whatever it may be—here I am. Just me—warts and all. And I'll take you like you are if you'll love me like I am." Then we'll gracefully reach out and find each other, and we'll make it together till help comes. That's grace. We'll make it together till help comes!

Stranded With Despair
Bill

It was the best of times, it was the worst of times
It was the age of wisdom, it was the age of foolishness
It was the epoch of belief, it was the age of incredulity
It was the spring of hope, it was the *winter of despair*
(Dickens, *Tale of Two Cities*)

*D*espair is living in a bleak city apartment on a rainy Sunday afternoon, and the phone won't ring.

Despair is feeling like you're in a dark room with no doors or windows.

Despair is that sick feeling in the pit of your stomach when you know you have disappointed and hurt your family.

Despair is the feeling you have when the doctor tells you there is no hope your loved one can live.

Despair is the realization that you're pregnant with your fourth child, and you only planned for three.

Despair is heaviness in your heart when you stand beside the grave of your husband or wife.

What the future holds is impossible to determine. The past pushes our imagination to an emotional overload—short circuiting reason and driving us beyond concern to perplexity and to the brink of despair.

Paul wrote to a Corinthian church in a turbulent and tormented world driven by the collapse of every system of support it had. He said: "But we have this treasure in earthen vessels, to show that the transcendent power belongs to God and not to us. We are afflicted in every way, but not crushed, perplexed, but not driven to despair" (2 Cor. 4:7-8, RSV).

Catch the feeling in those words—for words are understood as well by feeling as by analysis.

"Afflicted in every way (stock market decline, dollar devaluation, Watergate), but not crushed—"

"Perplexed, but not driven to despair—"

Perplexed—full of doubt or uncertainty—puzzled, hard to understand, confusing.

Despair—to lose or give up hope—to be without hope.

The key is that Paul was not driven to give up hope.

We have many reasons to be perplexed. Education has evolved from the one-room school, memorizing historical dates and plain arithmetic, to classrooms filled with electronic teaching aids, on-the-scene history lessons via Telstar, and electronic calculators for mathematics. Today's student has no time for reflection. Mere survival in some of our school systems is reason enough for a diploma. There have been serious emotional disturbances, family crises, and feelings of despair in both parents and children that can be traced directly to the decline of the public school systems. This is an acknowledged area of perplexity.

Our political complexities are mind-boggling. We have come a long way since George Washington said, "I cannot tell a lie." Where is integrity in the political arena? Where are our statesmen? Is it true that every man has a price?

Take a look at the spiritual fiber of our nation. For all of our advances in technical areas, we are religiously ignorant and spiritually empty. As the first century was in a religious vacuum, so is the twentieth; and the prophets of the cults, crusades, and cosmos rush in to fill the vacancy with spiritual husks. Electronic magic has produced in us the desire for immediacy, and this drives the religiously immature to want instant feeling with no time for growth.

Add your own personal despair to these social, political, and religious perplexities. Are we going to make it? Should we call off tomorrow for lack of interest? Do we have the moral fiber to stand or are we to be driven to despair—hopelessness? Now abideth faith, hope, and love, but greater than these is *despair*—some think.

We are like the men in the submarine caught in the mud

on the bottom of Boston Harbor. The men inside faced death bravely. The electric power was out, their oxygen was almost gone, and they knew the end was near. Their spirits rose when they heard the "clank" of the metal boots of a Navy diver as he touched down on the exterior of the steel coffin. Anxiously, the radioman tapped on the interior of the submarine. Is there any hope? The word came back from the diver, slowly and distinctly—yes, there is hope.

We cry for hope in the midst of circumstances that threaten us with despair. Is there any word from God? Is there any hope?

Yes, there is hope, because this is God's world. "The Lord God Omnipotent Reigneth." God created it, "and it was good." He sustains it. We have marked our lives with his hope signs:

At Christmas—he invaded it
　　At Calvary—he died for it
　　　　At Easter—he triumphed over its evil
　　　　　　At Pentecost—he empowered it

Our sense of immediacy does not allow us to remember what God has done. Israel was reminded often of the times of God's deliverance. Our memories are short. We cry like spoiled children—what have you done for *me* lately? He sends back that piercingly personal death warrant . . . For God so loved the world that he gave. . . .

We bury our heads in the sand—blind to experience and insensitive to pain. I am reminded of David's words: "Yea though I walk through the valley of the shadow of death, *Thou art with me.*"

Our electronic age makes us want a vending machine god. Put in your quarter, and get your immediate answers. The ages tell us: "Be still and know that I am God"; "I am with you alway(s)." John on Patmos, perplexed, saw a "New Jerusalem" coming down out of heaven. What God does revolves around his earth. The accumulated testimony of the ages is that he has not left you to the powers of evil.

There is hope because of God's church. That's right, his

church. That dead, provincial, empty, inert, obtuse place where you are guaranteed boredom. That organism everyone predicts will die—but will not. That outdated organization that serves itself (so they say) but keeps on plugging away at evil in season and out.

- The church was in the ghetto before it became acceptable. Ask General William Booth or Japan's Kagawa.
- The church was preaching and living brotherhood before the Supreme Court caught up to it.
- The church leaned against slavery, child labor, slums, war, hate, exploitation, and superstition before the current crop of activists arrived—and will continue long after the fad has passed.
- The church was in the education business long before the state thought about it—Note: Princeton, Harvard, Stetson, Mercer—and will be in it long after the government has grown tired of it.
- The church was providing community in the face of alienation and sanctuary in the midst of storm before "communes" and the "hip" community discovered it . . . and will continue.

When your life caves in—when your dreams crash, when you have spilled your first emotional blood, the church will be there to kiss your wounds and to wipe your brow. This gnarled old crusty institution knows and loves you and is the best thing God has going for him in this world. The church knows that you must bleed before you can bless, and she's ready to stand with you in the process. It's painful, but you're not much good until you've been through your Good Friday (bleeding) and experienced the Resurrection (blessing).

The church has endured Caesars, dictatorships, medieval feudalism, European monarchs, colonialism, Communism, managed economy, modern technology, Southern provincialism, and a youth quake.

We can be perplexed but not to despair—ours is an age

of birth pangs, the birth pangs of a new era. Not the age of Aquarius but the age of God's Spirit.

Not despair—but *hope!*

The church is not perfect, and your particular church may fall far short of meeting your needs. It is the only place in the world where people will accept you and love you just the way you are. The church is my family. Had it not been for the church, who knows what would have happened to my life?

I grew up in the old First Baptist Church of Delray Beach, Florida. When they had a business meeting, they argued all night over nothing. I have seen men of good will almost come to blows in a congregational meeting. It was agony for me, a young boy, to watch that going on. It should have turned me against the church, but it didn't.

Years later two deacons came to see my mother and me. This is what they said: "We've just had a deacons' meeting and the only thing we've agreed on in twenty years is the fact that your son is the only ministerial student our church has ever had. We don't know what to do with ministerial students so we voted to pay for his education through college and seminary." That was good news to me! Then my mother looked those deacons straight in the eye and said: "Thank you. We appreciate your confidence, but my son will work his way through school." Her judgment proved to be right, but I knew those people cared about me.

A number of years ago some of my minister friends came by my office one by one and said: "Bill, don't you know the church won't be in existence in another five years. God is working somewhere else now." I watched them parade out one by one.

I recalled the opening scene in *Gone With the Wind* that shows the big celebration at Tara. Suddenly the word comes that the war had started: the men don their beautiful gray uniforms, jump on their white chargers and ride off to war believing that they will return victorious. Then the scene changes and they are back at Tara; the ground is decimated, the buildings are down, and all the tradition has gone. A long red clay road stretches in front of Tara. The men who rode off to the battles of Vicksburg, Appomattox; those who had fought at Gettysburg, Shiloh, Bull Run, and all the others, start coming down the road. The slaves who would not leave were standing, helping the family in a social condition that had totally been torn down.

The proud Scarlett and the others see the men coming down the road and run to them. The men's clothes are tattered and torn, some have lost limbs, their bodies are full of lice, and their bellies are empty. The men are given food, clothing, encouragement, and affirmation, and sent on to south Georgia and Florida to their farms, and back to Alabama so they can begin to rebuild.

And so it has been in the last few years. I've seen my friends come back from wars. Those who said they were leaving are now knocking at the study door and quietly saying: "We've found out that the church is where it is. As far as we're concerned, it may be out of date, but somehow there is a long, deep tap root here that reaches to the eternities. It may not swing, but this is where it is."

I'm going to tell a story I love—a story about Zach. This is the nonbiblical version story of Zacchaeus, the unwritten part of the story of Zacchaeus.

After his conversion he and Mrs. Zacchaeus were doing quite well at Jericho, but Mrs. Zacchaeus was worried about one thing. She said: "Zacchaeus, what do you do? You get up every morning and leave and then you come back about the time I'm getting up. What's going on?" With tears in his eyes, he said: "Honey, don't ask me."

Days went by and she came to him again and said: "Now, Zach, I want you to tell me what you really do in the morning when you get up like that and go out before I get up." With tears coming down his cheeks, he began: "You know that old sycamore tree?" She said: "You mean that old gnarled, ugly tree outside the city?" "Yes," he answered, "you know that tree I was in when Jesus found me?" She nodded: "I know the tree." "Well," he said, "it's so old and ugly that I decided it needed a little care. I've pruned it, watered it, fertilized it, and now it's coming out a little bit." She said: "Why do you do that to that old tree, Zach? We've got a city planning department, the town council, and all those other things, why do you do that?" He said: "Honey, I don't know except that it is the tree that held me when Jesus found me."

The church held me through all those growing up years. Christ died for our church. He didn't die for that splinter group; he didn't die for your favorite charity; he died for the church. I believe in the "church universal," but Jesus talked about the church local—the church immediate—*our* church—this church—the family of believers—the gathered community. We face the future with a great deal of concern and apprehension, but we have two great strengths: the providential nature of a loving God who is underneath, above, and around, and the strength of his family of faith, his church.

Despair, no matter what the cause, is not hopeless. We belong to God and he loves and cares for us always.

Being stranded alone, in the middle, in sickness, or in any situation is frightening. You can survive. Remember that God will not leave you comfortless. One way God loves us is through his church, our family of faith.

We may be perplexed and stranded—but not to despair!

Stranded in the Middle
Bill

*B*eing in the middle is deadening. This is where people are for most of their lives. The danger of this position is that the defense systems we construct to survive lethal attacks can choke us to death.

Maybe you think you've never been stranded in this spot. Take another look—you must be so mutilated that the nerves are deadened, and you don't know you're bleeding to death. There are more of these "middle" positions available than at the top or bottom. Let me name a few so that you'll know what we're talking about: a child caught between parents; a wife or husband between spouse and parents; teachers between administration and students; students between teachers and parents; middle-age people stranded between two generations; middle income caught between the rich and poor; mother (or father) between spouse and child; and the list could continue indefinitely. These situations have always been operative as long as people have been able to manipulate and use one another—either intentionally or unaware of their attitudes.

Remember the Old Testament story of David and Jonathan? Jonathan was the sweet-spirited, gentle son of the angry, jealous, old King Saul.

Jonathan was a dear, close friend to David, who was obviously a rival to Jonathan's father for the throne. In every circumstance, Jonathan seems to be caught between his father and his dearest friend. The model of friendship between Jonathan and David is the highest kind of model of personal friendship.

Every time you read this story, you become impressed again with the fact that it seems as though Jonathan is a buffer between his father and his friend. "And Jonathan spake good of David unto Saul his father [See, Jonathan had to run to his dad and say, "Let me say some good things about David before you get angry"] and said unto him: Let not the king sin against his servant, against David, because he has not sinned against thee [He's pleading the case up there] and because his works have been to theeward very good: For he did put his life in the hand, and slew the Philistine, and the Lord wrought a great salvation for all Israel: thou sawest it, and did rejoice; wherefore then wilt thou sin against innocent blood, to slay David without a cause?" Here's Jonathan always caught between his father, the king, and David, the rival for the throne and his best friend, and he's being beaten between the two.

There are several ways that people get caught in the middle. Some people get stranded in the middle because of status, and I don't mean high or low. I mean just because of who you are and what you do for a living, you get caught in the middle. There was in *The New Yorker* magazine recently a cartoon that showed a typical, well-cared for house. It said out front: "The very middle class John Jacob Rogers lived here." I looked at that and I thought, *that's not very funny*, and later I turned back and looked at it again. That's very significant for some people. There are some people who in their middle years all of a sudden realize that they're not only middle-aged and middle-class and in mid-career and in mid-management, but they also know they will probably never be anywhere else.

You remember the television advertisement for *The Wall Street Journal* that showed a pyramid with men trying to climb to the top? They kept getting lopped off on the way to the top of the pyramid and only one got through. Well, I'm talking about that vast host of people who are somewhere between the apex of that pyramid and down at the bottom—those of us who get caught somewhere in the middle.

It's the man who at the age of forty realizes he's not going to be president of the company. The boss has a son who is going to be president of the company. The "man in the middle" realizes he's not going to be the sales manager for half the country. He realizes that he's never going to be a millionaire. He realizes that his sons and daughters are never going to be Ph.Ds.

Somewhere along the line the idealism of youth and the realism of life and what you have had as an ideal begin to grind against one another, and you come to grips with the fact that you have to take life as it's being dished out to you. Now that's painful. I know a man who, when he hit forty, spent three years trying to bring his idealism (and I don't mean idealism in the sense of moral ideals—I'm talking about professional idealism—his goals for himself) into line with his own talent, and he faced up to the fact that his talent would never let him realize the goals he had set for himself.

We were visiting some of our dear friends who live in another city. They said to me: "Bill, we've made up our minds that our children are just going to be average children, that's all. It's been a great burden that's been lifted from us."

There comes a time in a person's life when he has to accept the truth that he is who he is. He has to make up his mind what he's going to be; he has to make up his mind that he's going to accept whatever life has dealt to him. There may have been some bad decisions behind him; there may have been a bad marriage; there may be bad attitudes; there may be many factors that have come together to pull this person over into a middle section. But that isn't all bad. You can't have every man president of the company. Somebody has to do the work. That's true.

You know this old notion. If you're going to get anything done, go to the top. Nonsense! Call middle management. They run things. The man at the top doesn't know what's going on. He's planning. He's twenty years ahead. It's the guy in the middle that does the pots and pans work. American industry, American business, America is run by that great slice of people in the middle.

Many people who are caught in the middle somehow feel

as though they're caught in a bad situation for another reason. It's illustrated by the old airline fare we had. There was youth fare that went up to twenty-one, eighteen, or somewhere along there, and there was senior citizen fare. But everybody caught between twenty-one and sixty-five had to pay for both ends. Ralph Nader found out about it and changed it. (Wait until he's a senior citizen; he'll get it changed back.) The point is that the man in the middle gets caught from either end. He's not poor enough to get on welfare, and he's not rich enough to afford to be sick; so he's caught in the middle with heavy bills.

How do you live this way? Begin by facing up to the situation: this is where I am, and this is what's going on. Don't tie your life up this way. Whenever this realization comes, don't tie your life up there. You can develop a lot of new interests. You can get your job back into perspective and yourself into perspective and have a good, healthy understanding of who you are. You can also find some new goals in life. Maybe you had better start learning how to read something besides the funnies and the sports page. Perhaps you can start taking those trips that you've been putting off. Perhaps you can start coming to church more regularly.

Remember, you're not dead until you turn your toes up. Just because you're not going to make it to the top doesn't mean you're going to have to quit living. In fact, one of the happiest men I know is a man who one day decided that life was more than being a drudge at the office and a grouch at home. He decided he wanted to put his life into a situation where he could be something worthwhile and be a good human being. Tremendous excitement was the result.

Now let's turn the page from the middle status to an entirely different kind of being in the middle. It's the kind of being in the middle that's hard to describe, but it's something I see almost every day as a pastor. It's the kind of middle position that grinds people to death and makes hamburgers out of their lives. It's the kind of middle situation that causes people to develop a severe case of ulcers. It's when you get caught between two kinds of people.

As we were going into church supper one Wednesday evening, I asked one lady: "How was your trip?" I knew she had taken a little trip to another state to visit some relatives. She turned to me, focused both eyes on me very tightly and said: "I had to take care of my children and my grandchildren while I was there; they were caught in a bad situation. Then we had to get on a plane and come back quickly and go up to north Georgia and take care of my husband's parents."

I said: "That made a busy week." She said to me: "We didn't mind doing it; it did make a busy week." Then she sighed and said: "It's hard being caught between two generations." That's the kind of being in the middle that's tough because before you realize it, you get manipulated between two generations, and it's difficult to survive there. I make plenty of happy, but terse, remarks about grandparents and grandchildren having a lot in common—they both have the same enemy, the parents, in the middle. But the guy in the middle somehow feels as though he has to keep things balanced out, and it begins to grind in on him.

Another kind of "middle" I see is the parent who gets caught between a child and the world, between a child and his friends, or between a child and school. I have talked to principals who have been harassed by parents who want schools to bend laws for them. I have talked to parents who have been terribly upset because they cannot control every single minutia of social life. I have seen parents who want to stand between the child and any kind of rough experience.

I visited a home one night where there had been a death. This situation had a number of tragic overtones to it that do not normally accompany death. Everybody was running around doing the supportive things that people do. I noticed a fifteen-year-old boy—the son of the man who had died—and nobody was paying any attention to him. They were all caught up and going in another direction. I went over to this boy, called his name, and asked: "Do you want to talk?"

We went out and sat on the porch of that Florida home

for about an hour and talked about his father's death, the consequences of it, and how the boy felt about it. No brilliant stars came out; we didn't see or hear any thunder and lightning, there wasn't any great emotional thing going on there. But the next afternoon at the funeral, that boy came to me and said: "You made me feel like somebody cared about my feelings." You can't stand between people and emotional experiences. They have to grow in their own.

Another kind of situation in which I've seen people get themselves caught is being "helpful." A Christian gets excited about the idea of going out and helping somebody, but "helping" somebody sometimes can reach the point where people turn on you. If you don't believe it, the next time your neighbors get into a marital squabble, go over and tell them you're going to help them. Just go right on in—"I'm here to help." They'll turn on you. I've seen many people line up to support one side or the other prior to a divorce. I've seen people getting ready for a divorce try to line up all the help they can. They enlist many people in the middle and just grind them up. When it's all over, you've been turned into hamburger, and the other people go on. Now sometimes the best way you can help people is to let them help themselves. Give them support and strength and undergirding, but don't solve anything. They're adults; they solve things.

I've also seen people become caught between antagonists, and now I'm talking to Bill Self. The best way to illustrate this was when we were building our church in Florida. Great church; great building program; had a great time; we had a great builder and a great architect. There was only one thing wrong with the builder and the architect: they wouldn't talk to each other. I thought that was funny for a day or two, but that went on for a year and a half. The builder was determined to go into arbitration; the architect was determined not to; and I was determined to hold the church together.

The architect would fly in from Miami, and he would ask us to bring the builder on the site. The builder would come, and we'd be there and the builder would turn to me and he'd say: "Tell the architect thus and so." And the architect would say: "Tell him so and so." I did this about three times, and one day I stopped and said: "Wait a minute; you're standing three feet from one another and you're both adults. I'm just a young preacher, and I think you can talk to each other." They both turned on me right there.

To make sure the situation would go into arbitration, the builder, to stay inside the contract, placed one man on the job putting down molding around the church. Well, I didn't care what the man was doing. I merely wanted to finish the project because I had a congregation that said to get it finished. Well, this farce went on and on; finally, we got into the church about a year later than we should have been in it, and it almost put me in the grave. When it was over, one of our deacons said: "Pastor, here is my credit card; you and your wife get in your car and go. I don't care where or how long, just bring me the receipts when you come back."

When we were in Switzerland looking at . . . no, that was too good a line to pass up. Actually, we went to Winter Haven and spent a week. It wasn't a vacation; it was letting the wounds heal. I came out of that fiasco and I said: "I'll never get between people who are adults." Now the point is this, don't let yourself, in the name of doing something right, get ground up when people who are adults can grind it out between themselves. You have enough sense to know it, but I spend one third of my time telling people, "Don't get in there; that's not your responsibility."

The other day I was talking to a young lady who was going to get married, and she was all upset about her mother who was just really controlling things in the wedding. I said: "Honey, don't you know what's going on? It's not your wedding; it belongs to your mother. Now you put on your clothes and show up and let your mother have a good time." I talked to the groom just before we went in. He said: "It worked. We just put on the clothes and showed up and the folks are having a ball." I've seen a spouse try to get between their spouse and the in-laws and it doesn't work.

All right. What should you do? There you are—a right-thinking person, and you don't know what to do with your situation; you're carrying it on your shoulder, carrying it in your heart—what should you do? Well, first of all determine that God did not call you to go get in between people. I think Jonathan should have stayed out of the fight between David and Saul. He loved them both and it ground him to death. He ended up being killed. I think Jonathan should have stayed out of it, but Jonathan didn't ask me. I think that good, knowledgeable people have to come to the place where they understand where they should be and shouldn't be. I realize for ten years the Christian faith has been saying to everybody, "Get involved." I'm not saying, "Don't get involved." I'm saying get involved the right way. Get involved in a supportive thing, not as a buffer zone between two people who are beating themselves. Don't let other people play on your guilt.

People have called me and said: "Would you go out and tell my husband thus and so?" There were years in my ministry when somebody would call and say: "My husband and I are not getting along well; he's going to be passing by Manatee Avenue and Fifth Street at two o'clock; would you be there and talk to him? You could just happen to be on that corner when he goes by." I did that. (You know—here's the preacher hiding behind the bush ready to pounce!) I've done those stupid things. "My husband always goes to lunch at such and such a place; could you just happen to be there and just happen to mention that I think he ought to quit doing this or that?" I've done that thing, too. One day it occurred to me: that's not what ministry is. My job as a minister is not to let that lady or that man play on my guilt and make me feel responsible for what they've taken ten years to get into. Don't let others play on your guilt that way.

Another thing is that we have to learn to let others take the responsibility for their own actions and their own situations in the world. You cannot protect people from this responsibility or from these situations.

The last thing I would say to you who find yourself, like Jonathan, caught between a Saul and a David, is get out. Just get out. Strangely enough, when you step out, you'll find that you feel better, and they do better. Now these are broad, general statements to those of you who are caught in the middle of situations. How you apply them is up to you. Our job is to create mature people who carry their own burdens in a world that's filled with all kinds of bumps and grinds. There are times when we are supporters and implementers, but we do it in a way that activates personality and independence and not in a way that grinds up everyone involved.

Jonathan, Saul, and David found themselves caught in strange situations. I've often wondered what would have happened in the biblical situation if Jonathan had let David and Saul work it out, which they ultimately had to do anyway.

Stranded Parents
Carolyn

A young mother struggles with two babies—the oldest nearly three, the youngest about eighteen months old—trying to buy groceries, remain pleasant and calm, and avoid running the grocery cart into a display of canned goods. While waiting in line at the checkout counter, the oldest child makes unreasonable demands, refuses to be pacified, and pitches a super-duper temper tantrum. In despair, the mother hands the baby to the nearest motherly-looking woman to hold while she scoops up the screaming, kicking child, carries him to the car, locks the doors, and returns for the baby. Groceries left behind, she drives home vowing never again to take both children to the grocery store, even if the cupboard is bare!

A middle-aged father and mother sit in stunned silence as they realize that their teenage daughter has run away from home and is living with friends who are less than desirable.

A young couple lovingly bring their retarded, deformed child to Sunday School knowing that their son will never be able to be active and noisy like the children they see in the other preschool classes.

The telephone rings shortly after midnight and a mother's heart beats faster. Her daughter is late coming home from a party.

In another home, the parents of a teenage son are weary. They are bombarded continuously with unreasonable demands for "freedom" and privileges with no responsibility attached.

The divorced mother of two preschoolers rushes to dress herself and her children, feed them breakfast, get them to the day-care center, and herself to work on time; then finishes the day in exhaustion trying to make up for lost time with the children.

A mother, father, and fifteen-year-old son are involved in a three-way tug of war over the purchase of a suit for the son who doesn't want or like it. Everybody, including clerks and other customers, feels uncomfortable, and moves away from the war zone.

A sixteen-year-old girl flounces and pouts and flings cutting remarks at her cowering mother who cannot afford to buy her but one expensive coat. She doesn't mind the embarrassment she causes her mother and the other customers and clerks.

There is a man, graying at the temples and with slightly stooped shoulders, turning the key in the back door knowing the house is a turmoil of noise and people—but at least they love him.

These are not fictitious situations. The list could go on endlessly—you could make your own list. No doubt all of these adults who find themselves in the parental role once had dreams of the ideal family. Remember the old song:

> Oh, give me a home, where the buffalo roam,
> Where the deer and the antelope play.
> Where seldom is heard a discouraging word
>   and the skies are not cloudy all day.

That sounds great, and we may occasionally achieve that serenity, but huge chunks of our lives are spent trying to make the car, tractor, lawn mower, motorcycle, washing machine, dryer, dishwasher, and all other necessary machinery work; not hearing anything but fussing and nagging; and the cloudy skies may mean leaking roof or bankruptcy (no way you can save enough for that rainy day!).

Most of us who are middle and older parents grew up when "daydreams" were our best entertainment. These for the girls were built on stories of *The Five Little Peppers*, *Little Women*, *Pollyanna*, and that sort of nice and neat theory of life. The boys read something they could identify with, something both adventurous and heroic. Of course, we all lived happily ever after. The radio programs were fun and just dramatic enough to tantalize the imagination.

I don't know about you, but violence was not part of my life. My children grew up with violence via the cartoons on television. Most of our generation probably fit the pattern that was predetermined for us simply because we didn't know there was another way. Runaway teenagers are commonplace now, but how could I, living three miles out in the country or later in a very quiet neighborhood in a very quiet town, run away? Maybe I could have gone six blocks before someone would have called my mother to ask where I was going.

What I'm trying to say is this: Because of changes brought about by the electronic media and the crush of society, our dreams have been shattered. If we can keep our families from completely disintegrating, we are not so bad. "The happy homemaker" is busy helping to earn a living, driving car pools, figuring the budget, carrying a meal to a shut-in, teaching a Bible class, cleaning, sewing, and cooking. If you are upset because your husband is gone all the time and the children are subversive, just remember that this right now is just one piece of time and this stage will pass on to another. All you are required to do is the best you can with God's help. One piece of advice that my husband gives is very undignified but is to the point: "Keep both feet in the stirrups and don't spit in the wind!"

It is becoming more and more important to at least make an effort to have family traditions and customs. There may be times when parents are the only ones observing them, but the child will be aware that it's important to you. It will leave an impression that can be recovered later when he is ready.

At some point most parents feel helpless and stranded. For new parents it may be the night after day after night of walking and rocking a colicky baby, or that terrifying croupy gasp when you steam up the bathroom and call the doctor. There is some doubt as to whether mother is stranded or free on the day the youngest child starts school. As you grope your way through the adolescent years you *know* that you're stranded at least every other day! Grandparents are stranded, also, when they feel in depth the pain of their children and grandchildren.

Bill

The remainder of this chapter is a portion of a Father's Day sermon with which mothers can also identify.

Well, here we are on Father's Day again. It's interesting how the secular holidays can somehow push themselves into the middle of what we do in church and that we give a great deal of emphasis to Mother's Day and Father's Day. Neither of these holidays are part of the great tradition of the Christian church but they emphasize the fact of family stability and strength. As I approached the Father's Day situation again, several things pushed in on me. The role of mother and father in our culture is undergoing a tremendous change right now. Every sensitive family has felt the pressure of change.

As I looked over all the literature available to be read in preparation for this day, I was impressed again with the fact that about 95 percent of the literature written for Father's Day and Mother's Day was guilt-inducing. A father should be . . . and then you set up all of these things that not even Superman in all of his glory could do. Or a portrait of a godly mother or father with extreme patterns outlined. When I was a young fledgling minister, I would have said that all of us fathers ought to be these things. Now I want you to know that I'm the father of two teenagers, and I'm not about to set any kind of example for anybody. I'm just about to tell you how to survive and that's all. All you do as a father in this kind of day is just survive. The day you determine that you're going to be what "they" say you ought to be, somebody else is going to write a book saying you should be something else. Things are going to change. Now a man has to find out who he is and go in that direction, but the guilt-inducing nature of these holidays should not be our stance.

Several years ago, a man in his middle years came into my office. He was bruised from the grinding experience of being employed by a large company for twenty years. His eyes were bloodshot from crying. He said that a young, aggressive sales manager had come in, rearranged the territories, and had given him a small desk in the corner with one account to service. Then he focused his eyes upon me and said: "Pastor, I want you to know this is just about as close to being fired as a man can be without being fired." Another man said to me: "I have faithfully tried to serve my family and my company for twenty-five years. Now I'm getting near the time for retirement. I have a good record. I'm solid. I have done everything they've asked me to do. Now I find I am only seven years from retirement, and I have been fired, and I lose all of that."

The other day, I sat with a man whom I love dearly. He's been like an elder brother to me in the ministry. We sat across the table, and he was telling me some of the joys of his life; then in the midst of all that talking about joys, he turned to me and blurted out: "Bill, I am five years from retirement, and I've never really amounted to very much." Or the man who told me with tears rolling down his cheeks how his daughter had come back and said to him: "Dad, I'm sorry for those three years when I was really driving you crazy." They had embraced and had a reconciliation and then he said to her: "You're back, and you're sorry, and it's received, but I've still got a stomach full of ulcers."

A father in our culture is considered to be all kinds of things. Dagwood has said, and I've quoted him every year, "Fathers are a sorry lot." Then we come to church and find that we are to relate to God as though he's a father. The fathers hear this and all of a sudden they realize that their children not only learn what it is to be a man but they learn who God is because of their concepts of their father. That's heavy. That's almost more than you can bear.

I want to tell you about two fathers from American literature. The first father is familiar to all of us. His name is Willie
Loman. He is the central figure in Arthur Miller's play, *Death
of a Salesman.* The play came out in the mid-1940s, and it's
been a classic since that time. Anyone worth his salt has
found himself in that play. For thirty-four years Willie Loman
worked for the same company. He was a salesman and
worked Boston and New England. Willie was an empty,
shallow man. He was a man that believed that an ounce of
influence was worth a pound of performance. He never
performed but simply sought to give impressions. He was not
concerned about what he delivered, he wanted to keep his
image up. He had been caught in the old dreams of power,
prestige, and personality. Willie was quoted as saying: "If you
have class and connections, you can paint over your defects."
He was more interested in the *idea* of being a father to his
sons, Bill and Happy, then he was in *being* a father. When he
was away from the boys, he idealized them, but when he
came close to them, he panicked.

The funny thing about Willie Loman, the salesman, is that
we do not see the big hero who is undone by his own
bigness; we do not see the giant who finds that others don't
love him; but we see the shell of a man who all of a sudden
wakes up to the fact that he is the shell of a man. We see a
man who took all of his integrity and placed it upon the altar
so that he could have something.

One of the classic lines out of *Death of a Salesman* is
when Willie says that he would like to own something once
in his life before it wears out. Have you ever felt that way?
When you crank up your automobile, think about that. Willie
always felt that he could go through life on a smile and a
shoeshine. He had fantasized that when they had his funeral
that customers would come from all over the territory. But
there they stood by the grave: Bill and Happy, his wife, and
a neighbor. And the neighbor says of Willie: "Willie was a
salesman and for a salesman there's no rock bottom. Strange
thing about being a salesman: he does not put a nut on a bolt;

he does not tell the law; he does not give medicine; but he lives his life on a shoeshine and a smile and then he begins to worry when they don't smile back."

Now let's face it, fathers. Let's come right down to where you are. Is the shadow of Willie Loman flickering across you? The shadow of putting your integrity out on the line and swallowing stuff you don't like because you have to stay there; the shadow of knowing that you're an empty shell. It's tragic when you have to keep your integrity by making one more big sale or by leaping over one more tall building. It's tragic when your personal self-worth is tied to your achievements. If you have tied your self-worth to your achievements, you're never going to make it, because some day you're going to be a Willie Loman. There's nothing wrong with being a salesman. Half the men I know are salesmen, and the other half depend on salesmen. But there is something tragic about the man who has become the hollow shell. Now that's the death of a salesman, the death of a father. How do you bring a man alive?

Some men have tried to find new life by getting a mistress, only to find out it doesn't work that way. Others have tried to find new life by changing jobs. When I lived in Florida, many would come cascading in either when they retired or somewhere around their mid-forties. They sold out in Ohio, Indiana, and Michigan and moved to Florida only to find that hell was portable and the same empty shell they were in the North, they were in the South.

The most devastating but life-giving experience that any human being can have is when he is the recipient of graceful treatment; when he knows that his self-worth is not wrapped up in what he achieves and he realizes that people like him for what he is, not for what he achieves. How do you put new life in the old man? Let the old man know that you love him because he's a human being, not because he's a super salesman. The most graphic experience of grace I have ever received was during the period of time from '67-'71 when I labored long into the night and early in the morning on a doctoral dissertation in the area of hermeneutics.

The day came for me to hand in my dissertation which was *the* product of those years and my whole professional and, I thought, personal self-worth was caught up in that dissertation. I turned it in to my major professor and heard nothing, which was terrible. I knew that the thesis had to pass the committee before I went to the oral, and so I called him and he said: "I was just getting ready to call you." Now he *said* to me: "The first chapter needs to be rewritten." What I *heard* was: "It is not acceptable." I was in the bedroom talking on the extension telephone. I put the receiver down and all I heard was: "The thesis is unacceptable." I was stunned. I didn't know what I was doing because everything had focused in upon those pages. I walked into the family room of our home. I could not control my tears. I broke down in uncontrollable tears and for me to cry in front of my family was a difficult thing. I sat in a rocking chair in that family room and stared out the window almost oblivious to the fact that there was anybody else on the face of the earth. It was the lowest point of my life. Then I looked up, and there standing around me was a faithful wife and two children, not saying anything, not cheering me on like cheerleaders in the stand, not giving me injections of "think positive and get into the fight—you can do it" but just standing there, and by their action and some of their words (words are tragically inappropriate at times) they said to me: "We love you whether or not your thesis passed." They let me know that my position with them, my relationship in their heart, and my experience as a human being transcended anything I would ever write.

Late that evening I pulled myself together, found out that all I had to do was rewrite the first chapter, which was a major undertaking. I rewrote the first chapter, submitted it, and passed. But the passing of the oral examination in my doctoral program will never mean nearly as much to me as three people standing around me saying, "We love you." Now that's grace. When the church learns what grace is, we won't have to have these silly little games where people must achieve. When the church learns what grace is, all of those who have been dehumanized by our society are going to feel at home in church. When the church learns what grace is, we're going to see the gospel anew. We can articulate the fact that God loves us like we are, but when we can gracefully touch each other, old men are going to come alive again.

Another thing you can do to bring new life to the old man is to see him as a man, not as a salesman or a success or failure. It's interesting to me that the title of the play is *Death of a Salesman*. Wouldn't it be tragic to be born a man and die a salesman; to be born a man and die an architect; to be born a man and die a businessman? I want you to see that you are different from your profession. You are a person, not a profession.

I was playing golf ten or twelve years ago with a friend and his teenage son. My friend was the pastor of a church in a little orange grove town in south Florida. As we were waiting to tee off, the foursome ahead of us began to tease the son about his father being a preacher. One of the men in the other group said: "Son, is your dad a good preacher?" And the boy, with wisdom that transcended anything I have heard, said: "I don't know, but he's a super father." This boy was on it!

The character and integrity of Atticus in *To Kill a Mockingbird* stands in stark contrast to the empty shell of Willie Loman. This is a story I've told every year for the past seven or eight years—by popular request! It is from *To Kill a Mockingbird* by Harper Lee.

The setting is a town in the mid South during the late twenties. In the stillness of a hot summer you could feel the dust in your nostrils and hear the slapping of screen doors in that peculiar whang that's made by old porch door springs. Men sat around in front of the store and blew gnats; people spent the middle of the day out of the sun; you could hear the tick-tick-tick-tick-tick of a Ford automobile coming down the street; you could sit on the porch in the evening, sip your iced tea and hear your neighbors laughing or crying. During this summer in the deep South the two communities, the white and the black, lived with their stand-off relationship. Tom Robinson, a Negro laborer going to and from his work every day, walked by the home of a white sharecropper. The sharecropper was a family without much integrity but with a great level of frustration. The young girl of that home somehow involved Tom Robinson in a circumstance where he was innocent, but she claimed he was guilty. In those days in the deep South the Tom Robinsons had little voice in the official areas, especially when it came to defending themselves. Tom was slapped in jail; the judge looked around for someone to defend him, and he chose a man named Atticus.

Atticus was a good, county-seat lawyer with integrity and warmth, who was a widower with two children, Louise and Jem. The trial droned on. It was the only exciting thing happening in that county-seat town, and the people had already decided that Tom Robinson would have to be found guilty. But Atticus had made up his mind that the man was innocent and did everything he could to defend him. It was evident to the community that Atticus was putting his integrity on the line for Tom Robinson. The final day came, and the jury was to bring in their verdict. Everybody in the county came to hear the result of their deliberation. The downstairs of the little county-seat courthouse was jammed with the white community, and the U-shaped balcony was filled with the black community. In the middle of that group was the old black minister, who was the leader of his community. He was wise, powerful, and had plenty of sagacity.

Louise and Jem were late and couldn't get in downstairs, so they pushed their way upstairs. They stumbled over people in that balcony and sat right at the feet of the old black minister, pushed their feet through the banisters, let their legs hang over, and looked down into the courtroom. Louise had become wise in the ways of the courts and juries. Her father had taught her how to tell what the verdict would be; if it was "guilty" the jury never looked the defendant straight in the eye. The jury came in, each staring at the floor or the ceiling, and the judge called the foreman of the jury. He stood and called the name of each one in the jury and they all came forth, not looking at Tom Robinson, and said: "guilty," "guilty," "guilty." By the time it was over there was silence in the courtroom; relief on the main floor, pain in the balcony. The main floor emptied quickly except for Atticus who just stood there staring at the papers on the desk, shuffling them, and trying to put them in his brief case. The balcony was motionless; no one had moved. Then Atticus, unaware that there was anyone else in the courtroom, moved slowly toward the front door. As he walked slowly through that courtroom, the black community stood with him almost as though someone had given them the cue to stand as he passed. Louise and Jem were not mindful as to what was going on; they were caught up in other emotions. All of those in the balcony were standing as Atticus walked out, and then you could hear in the quiet, the stage whisper of the old black minister: "Louise, Louise, Miss Louise, stand up, stand up; your father's passing by."

Stranded in the Stained-Glass Jungle

Carolyn

I do not write this chapter without being aware that all professions have degrees of loneliness. The degree that this is felt depends on the level of sensitivity of the person and family involved.

Anyone who is a church school teacher, deacon, steward, elder (or the spouse of one of these), choir member, missionary society worker, or any of the volunteer jobs which require so many hours of service will recognize feelings that are embarrassing to acknowledge. Families of school teachers, principals, and public officials share many of the same experiences mentioned in this chapter. Because my husband is a minister, I am giving the view from the parsonage. However, I grew up with politics on the county and state level, and I know the two areas are closely related. If you are as honest as I dare you to be, you'll be glad to know that imperfection abounds—it is not limited to your family!

There are some ministers and their wives who have been able to make peace with their congregations by being the example of perfection that every one seeks. If this is truly the nature of the family, that is great. If, however, the family is made up of rugged, strong, independent beings, they cannot be controlled and made to hide behind a facade of perfection. I struggled with this for years.

This chapter requires complete honesty and openness on my part. I hope you can accept me, "warts and all," after reading this.

Several years ago the city of Atlanta was paralyzed by an ice storm. A few months later I was at a party listening to a woman relating in detail the difficulties her family had experienced during the storm. When she paused for breath, I murmured that we had also been without electricity. She looked stunned and said, "You mean the preacher had the ice storm, too?"

Not long ago my husband went into the grocery store with me (he likes to look at the gourmet foods occasionally), and a lady who sees him on television gushed, "I never imagined you have to buy groceries. You're in the wrong pew!" Or, the lady at the garden shop who heard us veto the delivery service on pine straw because of the added expense and said, "I guess you have to save money like the rest of us." Well, yes, we do have to skimp and save money. (How else could we survive?) And yes, we have ice storms and thunderstorms at our house. We have roofs that leak, TVs that break, toilets that overflow, lawns to cut, lawn mowers that break, shoes to buy, and too much month at the end of the money. Father *does* come home tired and irritable, mother *does* get tired of washing the same old dishes, the children *do* yell, and we use a lot of aspirin. Most of all, we *do* have feelings that can be hurt. Some people seem to take special pleasure in making unkind remarks to the minister at the door on Sunday morning. I guess it's like kicking at God or an authority figure.

The minister feels especially "boxed in" because there is no weekend time to "unwind." If he takes a day off during the week, there is the inevitable comment, "Must be nice to just work on Sunday." What fun is it to be off when everyone else is working? Someone always plans religious services for a holiday. It takes maturity and security to avoid being defensive. The minister is like the family doctor used to be—on call twenty-four hours a day, seven days a week. Each man has to decide for himself the value he places on study time. This is the most difficult time to claim. If a caller is told that the pastor is studying, he is apt to say that he'll only take a minute. That "minute" can break the whole train of thought or prayer, and Sunday's sermon is put off for another day.

Now to be perfectly honest, there are only rare cases of ministers who feed or care for each other. This is the area where ministers wear their masks and change characters for their own self-preservation. There is so much competition and gossip that no one dares admit to another that he is scared to death that his child is in trouble; or that he is so weary of raising money; he's worried about his own financial problems; or just plain "*Help!* I'm hurting inside." You have to know God called you to be a preacher, because once you're in, you're on your own where "the Brethren" are concerned.

This stained-glass jungle encases the parsonage also except that here the glass is clear and opaque. The stranded minister or staff personnel is a little different, because he or she was chosen of God for that. To some degree perhaps the wife also feels this calling. My personal situation was thus: I most decidedly did *not* want to marry a preacher or a chicken farmer. I just couldn't qualify for either one! But when I met Bill, I forgot to check on his career intentions because it really was almost love at first sight. I married the man, not the profession, and just as the wife of any professional man, I want to help him to be the best.

I think each wife has to find her best way to help. When children are little and underfoot just feeding, bathing, dressing, and keeping them out of mud holes until you reach the church yard is a major accomplishment and rates at least two stars in your crown if you scream only once. Some wives can give absolutely beautiful devotionals—now those ladies deserve something really special—because there are some of us whose hearts pound, tongues thicken, and who get sudden abdominal cramps when called on to pray in public. But everybody can be pleasant and kind, and that is most important of all. Develop a caring attitude toward people, and they won't care if you're not a prize package. After twenty-one years, I've decided that the thing I like to do best is the role of hostess. I'm so glad that my husband and our churches didn't make me be an assistant pastor. I'm Bill's wife and the mother of Lee and Bryan.

In many ways, the cover story in *Time* magazine, October 7, 1974, on "The Relentless Ordeal of Political Wives" is applicable to church staff wives. We do feel torn between the role we feel we ought to fill and the part that is handed to us. "She becomes public property, an extension of the public man, subject to unending scrutiny, judgments, accolades, and criticism."[1]

There have been very lonely times through the years and some very sweet times. It is important for someone to acknowledge openly the fact that all is not sweetness and light in the minister's home and family. You know that the physician's family is not immune to illness, and he is not expected to perform surgery on his own family. The minister's family should not be expected to be immune from the difficulties of just being human beings, nor should they feel a sense of failure when these difficulties seem to be over-whelming. Just because a person is a great counselor doesn't make him able to see what's going on with his own family. Or, he may be a great orator but no marvel at just plain conversation. (Who wants a sermon delivered on the spot when all he asked was, "Dad, can I go bowling tonight?") And then, of course, we also have the well-known "workaholic" minister whom Dr. Wayne Oates has identified for us. This disease attacks all professions and leaves devastated families in its path either screaming, writhing in anguish, or huddled in despair. I never will forget a friend whose father was a minister saying to me with some bitterness as a teenager: "We never just go anywhere. We always have to stop by the hospital or a parishioner's home even if it's not 'on the way.'" Think what it would be like on the mission field, isolated from family and friends, learning to cope with culture shock *and* a workaholic husband.

Women who are not even ministers' wives are attacked by the parallel disease which I have called the "helpaholic." She is the woman who knocks herself out doing good deeds for church, school, or community and has nothing left over for her family or husband. This gets to be a merry-go-round with no stopping point until priorities are established and she prac-tices cultivating the art of saying "no" pleasantly but firmly.

Helpaholics sometimes develop symptoms of illness as a way to cope with loneliness or as a desperate attempt to feel needed and acceptable. A good thing to remember is that we are doing a person a disservice when we do not allow him the privilege of doing for himself and the joy of learning new skills. There's just no point in being mother to the world! Those apron strings can choke you to death. What I really started out to say is this: Husband or wife, if you are lonely, discouraged, and hurting inside, don't suffer in silence and turn inward. Talk about it with your mate. It may not change a thing but at least he'll be aware of your feelings.

People frequently ask me what it feels like to sit in the pew and listen to your husband. It's something I just can't talk about. Sometimes when I am overcome with emotion— whether anger, rebellion, love, or despair—the only relief I can find is in exploding into words on paper. I am including two of these writings just as I wrote them at the time I felt so emotional. These express my deepest feelings and I share them, knowing that there is a great risk in emotional exposure, but possibly it may help in the growth experience of someone else who is feeling mutilated.

The first was written after a church conference to discuss adoption of the budget, including salaries.

Lonely Times . . .

After many years of living through church budget and planning and discussion, it is time for it not to bother me. However, last night demonstrated again the frailty of human nature and gross immaturity of young and middle adults. After hours and hours of labor and painful deliberation of the various committees, the desire to change something, anything, on the spot overwhelmed a few. To me it is like one who knows nothing about medicine and medical procedures arguing with the surgeon over a delicate operation. It is that stupid. Other analogies could be made easily to any profession or business.

What really bothers me is that I must finally acknowledge

that I am never more than display to anyone. I must at all times wear my mask, never exposing surface or deep feelings. There is never a time for really being free . . . not even family can understand unless they have also been in the same position. It would only upset them to know that I have feelings of resentment, or they would have difficulty being normal at church. They do not need any more concerns to deal with. What is most devastating is the cold fact that people only befriend us to use us. There are rare exceptions to this. These exceptions usually die.

One Monday morning while sitting in the orthodontist's office I was doing my usual thing—waiting—and instead of doing my needle point, I wrote down exactly how I felt.

What Causes Monday . . .

Maybe I am unique in that Monday dawns cold and gray for me almost without fail. Like today—actually it was a beautiful summer morning with a touch of cool breezes now and then, but when the alarm sounded and I had to make the conscious effort to shut it off, every muscle in my body shrieked out in protest. Today, strange as it may sound, even my fingers and toes feel almost numb; it is a real effort to do the necessary, commonplace things like pack a lunch for a son going to camp, focusing my mind on not burning the bacon, not getting the fried eggs too hard, pouring the coffee into the cup with a minimum of spillage.

This is sheer emotional exhaustion. It gets worse as the years go by because of the growing closeness between Bill and me. I am so aware of every feeling, every movement, everything that goes on in the worship services. When Bill exposes his emotional insides twice on Sunday, there is no way that mine are not exposed also. It is a weird experience—to be exposed but yet sitting in the pew. It is bearable if your people love you as ours do. There are many congregations where this would be disastrous and perhaps this is why there are so many "perfect" pastors. It is easier to wear a mask or veneer. Exposing the jugular vein can be suicidal without love on both sides of the pulpit.

It is easy for you to draw your own conclusions as to what this does to the entire family.

And then there was that Sunday morning in October of 1972 when the political campaign was waging hot and heavy and our clock radio woke us up with the news that got me out of bed in a fit of rage. Mr. John Erlichman, then the chief domestic advisor, made a statement about Mr. Nixon's opponent being the son of a minister that is so typical of the remarks made about parsonage children. That Sunday I couldn't wait to get home and write that man a letter. Several paragraphs from that letter are included here.

Mr. John D. Erlichman
Chief Domestic Advisor
The White House
Washington, D. C.

Dear Mr. Erlichman:

Your statement, "I remember very well when I was a kid that the minister's son was the biggest liar in class," lowered your political attack to unforgivable depths. Unfortunately, your statement is typical of the mind-set of unthinking people all over the world. (The doctor's son has a right to be ill; the coach's son can swing and miss; the chef's son can burn the toast; the attorney's son can get a speeding ticket; the minster's son is different.) Why? He was conceived and delivered into the world the same way all children are. I do acknowledge that the minister's family has more advice on all matters than other families. We get it in the form of unsigned letters, unidentified phone callers, subtle and not so subtle pressures. As parents, we walk a tightrope trying to deal with the rising resentment of our teenage sons, yet conscious of the role that is prescribed by society.

It is too bad that you didn't take time to do a little statistical research on the role that ministers' children have played in building our society. Did you ever stop to think why that minister's son in your class was such a liar? You obviously never accepted him as a fellow human being. If you never offered him your affirming friendship, you can be considered a contributor to his problem.

I realize that you made that unfortunate statement in the heat of political battle. However, not only did you participate in the character assassination of one man but of all clergymen across the country. It is hard enough to pick up behind a frustrated society without being stabbed in the back.

The children in the parsonage are unique in only one way—what people expect of them. They are generally expected to be smart, neat, well behaved, participate cheerfully in all church activities, and provide a model to whom all distraught parents can point. If by some miracle the child *is* a model, he surely won't be very popular with his peers. Many learn to play the game and wear the mask better than their parents.

Children react to parsonage life in as many different ways as there are children in the family. Some love it and move through adolescence with glorious gracefulness while others drag their feet and stumble and clumsily try to get their act together. It's no wonder some rebel when adult church members corner them and tell them what's wrong with the church and give instructions to their fathers through them. One son completely quit the activity program of the church when he had heard "OK, Preacher-Kid—get that ball in the basket" more times than he could take. (I didn't hear them yell "Doctor Kid, Salesman Kid, Builder Kid, etc.") For a sensitive child, it is painful to be different; to others it doesn't seem to matter. We were interested while talking to some missionary kids in Spain to find that these teenagers were very supportive of their parents' work and had very few negative things to say about their lifestyle. A great deal depends on the attitude of the parents, child, size and attitude of the community and the church, the type of school situation, and any other influence and pressures. There is a wide range between the normal rebellious teenager and one who goes off the deep end. One of my most memorable evenings as chaplain intern at Georgia Mental Health Institute was with the teenage daughter of a minister. I am including this case study because if you look closely, you will see the grief of both parent and child—each stranded and not able to reach the other.

I was chaplain on call Wednesday evening and was called to Unit 7 about six o'clock. When I got there, one of the nursing staff said that Susan had been very agitated, had tried to cut her wrist, was extremely upset, would not talk to any of the staff in that unit, and had asked for a chaplain. He gave me the basic facts about Susan: She is a teenage girl who had been there almost a year, had been home for spring holidays with her parents, and had come back rather upset. Her father is a preacher and she is one of four children. There seems to be quite a lot of family difficulty.

With these few words of preparation, he took me to her room where I saw three teenage girls and a room that looked like a hurricane had passed through. When he told her that the chaplain had come, the other two girls left the room very quickly, leaving Susan alone with me in the room. I sat down among the debris of the telephone book that had been torn up and everything else that was thrown around the room. I told her my name and that I was a chaplain intern. She just sat there and looked at me for a brief moment. She was sitting cross-legged on her bed Indian-style with a pillow which had the pillowcase off of it—she had torn the pillowcase to shreds. Her eyes were red and swollen and her lips were swollen from crying.

As the girls left, I sat down in the chair facing her. We looked at each other for a moment or two and finally she motioned toward the shredded phone book on the floor.

S. It's a mess, isn't it?

C. Yes, it really is. I'm glad you tore up the phone book and not somebody.

S. I've done that, too. I just want to die. I don't see any reason to live. Why should I live?

C. Surely you can think of any number of reasons to live. Tell me why you think you'd rather die.

S. One of my best friends was killed in an automobile accident about three weeks ago. I just feel so awful. I don't know what's wrong with me. (Then she looked at me accusingly.)

S. My daddy's a preacher and I hate him. I hate the church after what they did to us. We were run off from a church.

C. Did that have anything to do with you?

S. Yes. It was just a tiny little town—the people gossiped about us—me—my sister. Some of the things they said were true, but their kids were no better. I really was bad. I pushed dope in the church, and their kids bought it. Anyway, my daddy is two-faced. I used to be in church all the time. I'd hear my daddy preach and then see how he treated us, and I hate him for it. If somebody needed a dollar and he had one, he'd give it away instead of using it for what we needed. We did without, and that's not right.

C. Why did your father lose his church? Was it something he did?

S. No. They said they didn't have anything against him—just his family.

C. That's a heavy load you are carrying. You must be tired.

S. I sure am. That's why I want to die.

C. Is there anything else?

S. Yes. I had an abortion last year. They *made* me. I didn't want to have an abortion. My daddy wouldn't have anything to do with it, and my mother made all the arrangements, and they made me. I know I wouldn't have made a good mother but at least I could have given my baby life. I'll never forgive her for that. (She seemed far away in her thoughts and I waited—I didn't know what to say!) Finally I said:

C. Did being home last week make you think of all those

things again?

S. Yes, and my daddy has been sick and is a big baby and cross. I don't believe like he does, and he argues with me.

C. Tell me how you differ.

S. Well, I don't believe "once saved, always saved" and he does, and I do believe in speaking in tongues and he doesn't. I go to another church, and I'm comfortable there. I get scared when I think of all those awful things I used to say about Jesus. I was really *awful*. But I don't see why people have to keep throwing up things to me. Why can't they forget?

C. I don't think it matters too much about the religious issues you and your dad disagree on. That's not what is important. What is important is why you are feeling so awful right now. What are you *really* feeling?

S. Guilty—I feel guilty.

C. In your religious experience, do you believe that you can ask God to forgive you?

S. Yes, and I have, but I still feel bad.

C. If you were really sincere in asking for forgiveness, remember that in the Bible we are assured that God puts our sins as far from us as the East is from the West. He has wiped the slate clean for you, but you have to forgive yourself and stop thinking of yourself as bad. (She seems to be thinking about this.) When you have a bad cut, a scar is left after it is healed. It never completely disappears but it fades as time passes. It takes time for your emotional scars to fade.

S. I really am a mess. I've been in this place a year, and I don't think I'll ever get out.

C. Do you want to get out?

S. I don't know. (Long wait.)

C. Susan, I've been thinking about your dad and I don't like to sound "preachy" but let me help you see him differently. First of all, about his being sick—you know that men make very uncooperative patients—they require an enormous amount of attention—so baby him a little when you're home.

S. I guess I shouldn't argue religion with him—it doesn't make either one of us change anyway.

C. I wonder if maybe your parents are carrying a heavy load of guilt, also. They wonder what went wrong. They want to see you well and whole again, and they don't know how to help. They are probably just as frustrated as you are.

S. (Surprised.) You really think so? (I nod yes.) I never thought of that. (She heaves a great sigh—long wait.)

S. Boy, just look at this mess—and look at my mirror. I broke it and I use that when I put on my makeup.

C. I believe you'll have to invest in a new one or have lopsided makeup! (We giggle.) It's my favorite time of day, and it's so lovely outside. Do you want to go for a walk?

S. You mean you'll go for a walk with me?

C. If you want me to. (She nods.) Well, let's get this mess cleaned up so that when you come back you won't have to face it.

S. I guess that's a good idea.

(We filled the trash can and stood in it to press the trash down. I also found shatters of the mirror and glass. We stopped by the nurses' station and told them we were going for a walk. Susan wanted to walk down by the duck pond. It was a very easy, companionable feeling.)

S. This is where Joe and I used to come and smoke pot. We climbed the fence and hid behind the bushes. (She says this with a "see how bad I am" glee in her voice and face.)

C. How many times did you get snagged on the barbed wire? (She laughed and assured me she didn't do that now.)

C. What do you like to do when you go home?

S. Oh, I like to sleep late, and I may get stoned.

C. Why do you like to get stoned—what feeling does it give you that you like?

S. I just feel like I'm outside myself and I laugh at myself. It's fun.

C. I'll bet that really bugs your parents.

S. Yeah—Sometimes my mom is awake when I come in and she says: "Susan, what am I going to do with you?"

C. What would *you* do with you if you were in her place?

S. Spank me, I guess.

C. Would that do any good?

S. No. But I wouldn't want my kid smoking pot or doing acid or anything like I did. (Pause.)

S. What denomination are you?

C. I really hesitate to tell you, Susan, because you'll label me—Baptist.

S. Do you have to wear a hat to your church?

C. I haven't worn a hat in years and the only ones I've seen lately are either on teenagers or real old ladies. The way you're dressed now would be just fine at our church.

S. Really? You're kidding! Slacks in church?

C. You should see what walks down that aisle—it's really wild. Faded jeans with patches, pants suits, pretty dresses, boys with long hair, beards—young, old, pretty, and not so pretty.

S. My daddy's church doesn't allow long hair and jeans.

C. Well, you know long hair and jeans are personal things, I guess. You know how long my sixteen-year-old son's hair is? Almost to his shoulders. (Her eyes pop in disbelief.)

S. Do you like it?

C. Well, he has beautiful, wavy, golden hair, and the girls love it; it's important to him now, and I try to remember that. I really don't like it that long—I'd like it just below the ears. But I can stand the hair if his attitude is right.

S. That's really something.

(When we returned to her cottage she was all smiles and the nursing staff wanted to know what had happened. I found it hard to tell them in twenty-five words or less! This was an in-depth feeling situation, and it just so happened that we could really communicate.)

I cannot give you a happy ending to Susan's story. Maybe years from now she can get it all together. This type of situation can and does happen in anybody's family. To those who have been blessed with cooperative, well-adjusted children, just be thankful, and be careful not to pass judgment.

It is a consoling feeling to look around in our churches and see the active deacons, teachers, and leaders who are the products of parsonage life. It's good to know that most do make it.

It is hard to imagine what a child experiences through the years as he views his father from pew to pulpit. It must run the complete gamut between pride and embarrassment, particularly in the teen years when seated with his peers. It could be a very uncomfortable position.

[1] *Time*, October 7, 1974, p. 15.

Stranded at the End
Bill

*H*ave you noticed that a teenager will never commit himself about going anywhere until he takes a poll of his peers to make sure they're going to be there, too? The thing he fears most is to be *here* when everybody else is *there*. Most people in some category of their life feel as though they were left standing in the wrong line. Because of illness, vocational limitation, death of a loved one, wartime experiences, separation from family, or whatever the circumstances may be, they feel stranded. This condition is severe and widespread.

You can be stranded at the end of childhood; at the end of adolescence; end of a marriage; end of a job; end of a project; and toward the end of the span of life.

Now the end of things is not nearly as exciting as the beginning of things. In our culture, we have come to the place where we have placed a lot of emphasis on the beginning of things: the beginning of a new year; the beginning of a new life; the beginning of a new project. But the end of an era is something that you stand and look at critically. The end of a project is something that you breathe a sigh of relief when it's over. You've done a good job, and you're ready to go on to other things. The end of a life is something that's always met with sadness, and many people cannot handle it. Sometimes people find themselves at the end of things and cannot move from one time to another. The first category of these things at the end is the end of childhood.

The end of childhood is looked forward to by the child. He desperately wants to be that magic age of thirteen and then sixteen. Children are pushed and rushed into adolescence by parents and schools without having time to internalize all the phases of learning experience. Childhood has been exploited. The move from childhood into puberty is in many cases catastrophic, and our society cannot find the proper way to deal with it. We somehow forget that the capability and copability of the adult is the result of his childhood and adolescent experience.

The late adolescent usually decides that he has a good thing going and wishes to extend the combined delights of childhood and adolescence on and on. There are many young people who come to the end of adolescence and have difficulty becoming an adult.

There was a time when, if a young lady was not married by the time she was in her late teens, she was considered to be an unclaimed blessing. There was a time in our culture in the mid-nineteenth century when a young man in the late teens was focused in, married, started his family, and was ready to go. But we have extended adolescence. Now, if you work it right, you can go to college and not be considered really ready to do anything until you're twenty-two. If you go to graduate school, you can extend it until you're twenty-five. If you change your major two or three times, that means you lose two years and start over. When you're just about to finish up being a sociologist, you can decide to be a physicist and start over again. Keep doing this and you can stay in college the rest of your life. Dad pays the bills and you don't have to become a responsible adult. You can become the senior citizen of your fraternity house, but you have extended it as long as you can. Everybody tells you that you're supposed to be having the time of your life. It's more fun being a teenager; it's more fun being in late adolescence than any other time and you keep saying, "Is this all there is?" If this is when you're going to have the most fun, the rest is downhill all the way.

There comes a time when you have to step off the adolescent dock and get on the adult boat and start your journey, and that's hard to do—terribly hard to do. Some of you have done it. You've said, "I'm going to be an adult." You step into the adult world and get going and then all of a sudden you want to be a child again. You can't live in both worlds. I had a heavy, heavy dose of euphoria when I was in college. I'd preached in revivals when I got to college. I had preached almost every Sunday when I was in high school. And when I got to college, it was a revival every week somewhere. It was something special back in the Fifties to be able to preach a revival meeting at the Central Baptist Church in Miami, get on a plane Monday morning after a great evening service and fly up to Stetson University just in time to inform your professor that you just flew in from a big revival in Miami—that's heavy, man. I tell you, there's no life like that. The state executive secretary called and said: "Bill, would you address the Florida Baptist Convention?" I went to Tampa and addressed the Florida Baptist Convention which was meeting at the First Baptist Church. It was pretty heavy stuff, and I believed I was that good. I went to seminary, and the same thing happened at seminary. They came and put the red carpet out there—Bill Self has come to grace us with his presence! I had revival meetings all over North Carolina and Florida. I enjoyed every minute of it. I wouldn't saddle myself down with a country church. My wife was teaching school and I could afford not to take a church. Then that day came. The day came for me to graduate from seminary and do you know what I discovered? There wasn't a five thousand-member church in the Southern Baptist Convention that wanted a twenty-five-year-old ex-youth evangelist! The hardest days of my life were those last three months at seminary and the first three months after graduation when I had to make up my mind I was going to quit being a ministerial adolescent and start being a ministerial adult. I'd lived on about seven or eight sermons for seven years. Now I had to start shelling out every week, leading and feeding people whom I would learn to love. That's tough. So after having been honored and showered around the country, I went to a church of a hundred and eighty-seven members.

The building was so bad that my wife and I could not

wear our good clothes on Sunday. I learned more theology that first year than I learned in seven years of education or later in four years of graduate school. It was tough. There comes a time when you have to step off that glittering island of being an adolescent, because you can't cause that to linger for the rest of your life. You have to be an adult sometime, so put an end to adolescence and quit crying because life doesn't roll over when you throw a temper tantrum at the office, and they don't respond like mother did. Learn that you can't control the world any longer with your emotions the way you did at home. Just because you're a cutie pie or a favorite son at home, this does not mean the world is going to see you as cutie pie or favorite son. That's the hardest lesson, and some refuse to learn it. It's a hard step to move from adolescence to adulthood.

It is also hard to end the "productive, working years" and move into retirement. I worked in Bradenton, Florida, as the pastor of the West Bradenton Baptist Church for four wonderful years. Bradenton, Florida, is the geriatric capital of the world. We had more hearing aids and arthritic knees in our congregation than you can imagine. They were delightful, marvelous people. I came to appreciate their wisdom and experience and I learned a great deal from them. The very fact that they could tolerate someone as young as I was to be their pastor gave me great courage. Those people had worked all their lives for the magic year of sixty-five when they could retire and go to Florida. They sold their homes in Indiana, Michigan, all over the north, and came down to Bradenton, Florida, and put everything into a little trailer there. All of a sudden they became retired. For six months they would hunt, and fish, and play golf, and then they suddenly realized that it wasn't much fun being retired.

A retired executive from IBM came to our house one day and said, "I know you're the pastor of the church and don't have time to work in your yard. Let me do it. I'm about to go crazy around here with nothing to do!" I said: "I wouldn't feel right having you work in my yard." He said, "All right, if you'll let me work, I'll do it for forty cents an hour!" I would brag occasionally about having a retired executive working in my yard. But I always saw the sadness in his eyes as he worked.

A funeral director called me and said: "Bill, this person who has died has no connections down here, but would you come and do this funeral?" I went to the funeral home to do the funeral and you know who was there? The funeral director, pastor, and two people. I thought, how can life be so cruel when one has lived her years and she comes to the end of it and there are four people there. Two of them had to be there because of their official relationship.

Now, young people, we have desecrated old age enough in this culture. We have made people who find a few gray flecks in their hair feel as though there's something immoral about getting old. We've made people feel that they have done something evil just because there may be a few creaks in their muscles. That's not the biblical position. If you read it closely, you'll see that the Bible elevates old age. It is a place of wisdom and honor. It is not a place of derision; it is not a place of scoffing. The young say, don't believe anybody over thirty; I say, don't trust anybody under forty. They haven't bled enough; they haven't lived enough; they haven't died enough; they haven't had their fingers mashed enough to know what life's all about. As a culture can, we make those who are aging feel wrong. The Chinese honor their elderly, honor their wisdom. We're more like the Eskimo. The Eskimos put the old people on a block of ice and let them go out into the current to die. We can't even do anything that honorable at times. We get all tangled up in trying to do it. We let them come alone and enjoy their retirement in their old age with no money, no health, no freedom, no family, no respect, and no responsibilities. They've waited all their lives for this time, only to find that their spouse did not live as long as they did and because of that they have no status in the community. The youth emphasis brings disrespect. I've found that it's easy to raise money for youth programs but difficult to raise money for adult programs. The biblical view of old age is a reward for the good life. The modern view of old age is that you're sinful for living so long taking up my space.

What do you do about all this? First of all, whether you're an adolescent refusing to grow up or whether you're a person facing Social Security, face up to it. If you're an adolescent, just face up to what's going on. You're afraid to grow up, but you've got to grow up. You're going to look funny hanging around the malt shop at forty-five—or wherever it is that you hang around. Define your problem and face up to it. If you're an adolescent, you're going to grow out of it. If you're an older person, face up to the fact of age. I don't think any of us ever feel as old as we are. On Mondays I feel ten years older than I am! But during the week I don't, and on Sundays I don't. Occasionally I read in the paper where someone is referred to as being forty-two and I think, how old! Then I remember that I'm "that old" and I think, well, he's older than I am. I face up to the fact that I'm in those comfortable middle years, and I don't have to prove it any more.

The second thing I would suggest is for the adults. Don't accept the responsibility that belongs to adult children. I see more people who have waited for the golden years when they are free of responsibility. Their children are off and on their own and they have some time together and all of a sudden, the children dump responsibility back on them. Daughter or son gets a divorce and moves back in. They're not able to manage their lives so they send the children back to the grandparents. Whatever it may be, they just dump all this back on the adults, and the adults take it and prolong their adolescence. Now I'm not telling you how to run your home, but I'm telling you that part of developing mature children is to let them carry their own problems.

Now the third thing is, take a good, hard look and determine that you're not going to carry responsibility that's not yours. Make the hard decision. It is like the young girl who says: "I want to break up with this boy, but I don't want to hurt his feelings." You can't break up without hurting feelings. Any human relationship that has moved to a responsible basis from an irresponsible basis has some wrenching experiences in it. Adults, you're going to have to do some hard things as you talk to your children. Children, you're going to have to make some hard decisions about your life. It is said of the prodigal son in the Bible, "when he came to himself." The feeling of that verb phrase in the Greek is that he got over his emotional irresponsibility. It's almost a mental health term. Some of you are going to have to come to yourselves, and get on with it.

The fourth thing I would suggest is: take the pieces of your life and make something beautiful out of them. That sounds very ministerial. There's not a person anywhere who has a perfect life, and if your life has been perfect up till now, it's going to be imperfect somewhere down the road. It's going to have some bends and chinks in it. It will be in trouble somewhere. I hear a lot of people who divest themselves of being a happy person because something bad happened to them. There was a tragedy, my plans didn't work out and, therefore, poor little me. Well, a lot of people have had enough happen to them to make them "poor little me."

You know, stained-glass windows are only pieces of glass that have been broken and put together to make beautiful windows. There are beautiful mosaics where they take broken pieces of tile and put them together in patterns and make them worthwhile. In fact, the most beautiful things are made out of broken pieces.

Now the last thing I want to say is probably more for the young than for the old. Let me tell you how to have a happy retirement. Start planning for it now. I've made up my mind what I'm going to be like when I retire. We had a man in our church in Florida who was a great fellow. When he retired, he moved into it gracefully with style. He didn't start acting like he was twenty years old or even thirty; he acted just like he was sixty-five, but he enjoyed life. He traveled when he needed to travel. When he stayed home, he did the things at home that he needed to do, but he enjoyed life. He did not quit living. He had a full, beautiful, marvelous life. He kept up with the proper styles in good taste and so did his wife (they didn't look like 1920 and left over). They came by to see us the other day. They're getting up into their mid-seventies now, but they're really delightful people. I think it's Dylan Thomas who says, "go not gentle into that good night." Go into age screaming and kicking all the way, but when you get in there, make it what you can. If you're going to have a happy retirement, you better start now because I'll guarantee you one thing: when you get to be sixty-five, you don't become instant beautiful, instant nice, and instant sweet. You know the grandmother image. If grandmother has been a sourpuss for sixty years, she doesn't instantly become a lovely person when she gets to be sixty-five. She becomes a delightful, graceful sourpuss. And if she's been sweet and nice all of her life, she becomes even sweeter and nicer.

Your personality is not going to change that much; so you'd better start getting ready for what you're going to be. I found that the people who went into retirement best were the ones who made long-range plans. They had long-term life goals. They realized that God was in their lives, and they didn't stop living in certain interims. They got ready for it. Start preparing now not only financially (there are a lot of people to help you do that), but emotionally, psychologically, and spiritually. I wish and pray that we could harness all of the energy of those who have hours to give and yet for some reason think they're on the shelf. Prepare for the end now—not at the end.

I don't know where you are in your pilgrimage. I trust by God's grace that we'll change our attitudes concerning age and understand that God has something for every age with man.

How to Survive:
True Faith and True Grit
Carolyn and Bill

*I*n thinking about all the areas in life when we experience that awful stranded feeling, we want to offer something to give you courage. There are basically two things you need to survive: true faith and true grit.

True faith sets the tone of life. Whether your life is a continuing storm or relatively calm with appropriate clouds and rain to grow depends on your faith in God. The way we struggle through difficult times is determined by the depth of our love for God. Only he can be aware and concerned about each person in his world.

The writer of the Song of Solomon talks about the south wind and the north wind and the effect they have on our lives. The south wind brings sustenance and strength; it brings warmth and causes growth. The south wind is to be expected. I am sure the writer was thinking of the gentle breezes that come up from the southern part of Palestine, sweep across the Nile river, across the desert and over their farms. He also said: "Come, O north wind." He was talking about the shrill, north winds that blow from the tops of the mountains around Lebanon and chill to the bone. He declares that you must have the south wind and the north wind if gentle spices are to come. We need both winds in our lives. Most of us are willing to accept the south wind. We are always glad for life to be easy, to hear good news, to enjoy happy experiences. But we are not too happy when something causes the cold wind to blow across our lives.

Life is made up of an interplay of south wind and north wind. The north wind is sure to blow. Everyone has trouble.

We feel as though we are carrying just about all we can bear. If we have to carry anything else, whether it be emotional, psychological, physical, or financial, we will have more than we can bear. Most of us spend our times standing at the fence looking over into the other pasture. Our neighbor's grass is greener than ours; his swimming pool is larger; his car is bigger; his children dress better. We think everything is better somewhere else. Why should we have all the trouble?

We think that all of these burdens we carry are written on a large billboard in front of our house so everyone may see them. Actually, nobody knows about them but our own family. Our humanity causes our problems.

Even though we've been able to veneer over them, dress them up nicely, and smile through them, down deep inside the common bond that holds humanity together is the bond of trouble or north wind. Strangely enough, these troubles— north winds—should be the things that unite us, but they have become the items that separate many of us. It takes more than good fortune to make a life. You may think that you could stand a little south wind because you've had all the north wind that you can take. The north winds are the ones that really develop the individual.

Let's call the roll of history to see what the north wind has done:

Homer. If you were to list one of the two or three best poets who ever lived, you would have to include Homer's name. This blind poet was able to put on paper feelings and insights, understandings of life, that no other poet could capture. He put into words what it was like to smell the salt breezes that came across his life. Yet this man, blind, had more insight than most people.

Dante was exiled from Florence and was a wanderer. Milton said of him: "He speaks the voice of thirteen silent centuries. There goes a man who has been in hell."

John Milton in *Paradise Lost* was able to externalize the feelings that he had because of the agony of life. As he lived through a jealous home, blindness, and imprisonment that would have driven most men mad, John Milton was able to triumph.

Rembrandt. When you see his work, you come to understand something about his life. For you see, Rembrandt was poor beyond description. Most painters were able to afford some cloth to wipe the brushes on. But Rembrandt was so poor that he had to take the brushes that he used (and they themselves were of inferior quality) and wipe them upon his own trousers, for he had nothing with which to clean them. Yet Rembrandt was the one who gave us such brilliant masterpieces.

Syngman Rhee, the premier of South Korea, who for forty years was in exile. Seven of these forty years he spent in prison, and for seven months his captors beat him twice a day with bamboo rods, trying to break his spirit. It has been said of him that there has been no man in modern history who suffered more than Syngman Rhee.

At Warm Springs, Georgia, there is a marvelous shrine to a president of the United States who did great things for this country. Our family was there several years ago; and as we walked over the grounds, I was impressed that this man who had a body crippled by polio determined that he would not accept an existence that would make him only a custodian of his family's wealth. Rather, he determined that he was going to develop all that he had—*Franklin Delano Roosevelt.*

There is no better example of those who have endured the north wind than Paul, who said: "Five times I was beaten with thirty-nine lashes (forty save one, he calls it), three times I was beaten with rods, one time they came to kill me by stoning, three times I was shipwrecked and I spent a night and a day on the high seas, I have been thirsty and hungry" (2 Cor. 11). "I want you to know that what has happened to me has served to advance the gospel" (Phil. 1:12). "We rejoice in suffering, knowing that it produces hope" (Rom. 5:3-4).

The winds blow across our lives. Faith does not make us immune to the blasts of the north wind. The rain falls on the just and unjust. You cannot survive the north winds without a framework of faith.

What are you going to do with the cold winds that blow across your life? You must determine the kind of attitude you're going to have toward the winds. I read this review of a novel that describes the endurance Paul talks about.

"*True Grit* is when you are a fourteen-year-old girl from Yell County, Arkansas, and you've just shot a dangerous outlaw and the gun's recoil has sent you backward into the pit, and you are wedged in the pit and sinking fast into the cave below where bats are brushing against your legs, and you reach out for something to hold on to and find a rotting corpse beside you and it's full of angry rattlesnakes, and then it turns out that you didn't kill the outlaw, he's up at the rim of the pit laughing at you, about to shoot—and you don't lose your nerve. That's *True Grit*."

There comes a time when the only thing that will get you through is the fact that you just have to have grit, a synonym for courage. Courage is a missing ingredient for many lives. The only way you can endure the cold, brittle, hard north winds that cut to the bone is to develop internal *true grit* that will brace you.

True grit is a family standing by the bedside hearing the word that the operation has not cured the problem. A doctor, with all the professional integrity that he can muster, tells the family honestly what's going on. As you stand there with them, you see in the doctor's eyes that emotion that wishes he didn't have to do this. You feel the emotion from the family. The doctor leaves, and you see the family gathering up their religious faith to fortify them instead of railing against the universe. That's *true grit*.

You're a young person, somewhere around eighteen or twenty. One day you wake up and realize the world is not perfect. Somebody has sold you a bill of goods. They forgot to tell you that there are myths in this world, and you find out that they are not literally true. False grit sends you out to tear down everything like a child throwing a temper tantrum when his Christmas toy won't work. *True grit* says you work intelligently for change inside.

You're a young adult somewhere past twenty-five and not quite thirty. You've been hung in a marriage about seven years and you've passed out of the honeymoon—moonlight and roses—to the daylight and dishes stage. One day you look into the mirror, see a gray hair and a few wrinkles, and realize for the first time that you're not the belle of the high school ball, and your husband is not the football hero any longer. False grit says: "Well, I'll go out and live like I have no time left. I'll try to prove to everybody how lovely and feminine I am by throwing my morality away." *True grit* accepts yourself as you are and understands that you're growing up, and every stage of life brings a new kind of insight.

You're a young adult who realizes that on the surface it looks like the boy you turned down in college has turned out to be the best catch after all. You're caught with the one that didn't turn out so well. False grit says: "Well, I'll tear up everybody's marriage." *True grit* says: "I'll see the choices I've made and live within these choices and make the best life I can."

You're a young mother—at least you feel young. One day you realize that your husband is not the kind of man you wish he would be. Because of frustration in his own life, he is determined he's not going to be faithful. There's a sweet, young thing at the office who has nothing to do but put on eye shadow and buy new clothes. False grit says: "Just give up, become a shrew, nag him until he wants to leave. You'll have some legitimate reason then." *True grit* says: "Hold life together, hold it together because you know that in Christ you're going to bring your adolescent husband through."

You're a parent—a frustrated parent—who has read all the books on being a parent. One day you realize that your children are not going to be all that you've dreamed they would be. They have minds of their own, and because they're related to you, they're going to be something rather ordinary. False grit says: "Be cynical about it or goad them into being what they shouldn't be." *True grit* says: "Love your children, play with them, and accept them for what they are."

You're a parent who receives the word that because of an incredible series of circumstances, the death angel has come into your life. You feel like somebody took a baseball bat and hit you in the teeth. False grit takes out the fist and says: "God, why have you done this? I'm not going to believe in you." If you will be honest, you know that there are times when you have felt just like that. You wanted to reach out and strike at God and then you felt guilty about it. *True grit* just digs in, faces life, knowing that God has promised to bring us through even this.

Or your church, growing very fast, needs a new building desperately and doesn't know how to get it. You do all that you know to do and find out that it's going to cost you a quarter of a million dollars more than it should. False grit just gives up and says: "Woe is me." *True grit* says: "Tell the people, raise the money, and do what God has asked you to do—trust him."

In the top of the Alps are those little gnarled trees that are tough. The Alpine guides told us that these trees can stand anything. Up there it's cold and hard, but they're tough. In the valley you see the beautiful trees and flowers, but when winter comes, those green flowers and plants die because they can't stand the cold wind. But the gnarled, tough trees stand.

Kipling wrote a beautiful poem called "If." Part of it goes like this:

> If you can force your heart and nerve and sinew
>   To serve your turn long after they are gone,
> And so hold on when there is nothing in you
>   Except the will which says to them: "Hold On!"

* * *

> Yours is the earth and everything that's in it
>   And—what is more—you'll be a Man, my son!

I know the burdens that many of you are carrying. Some of you have seen your careers get a ceiling put on them. I know that many of you have been hit in the face with that baseball bat. For me to glibly say that the cold winds develop the inner man is not easy. But I can tell you that God says over and over again, in one way or another, "Yea, though I walk through the valley of the shadow of death, I will fear no evil, for thou art with me." It means that God is in that situation with you, and he is developing a real person with character as he sees you through it.

"Awake, O north wind; and come, thou south; blow upon my garden, that the spices thereof may flow out."

Afterthought
Carolyn

*P*utting this book together has been an interesting experience for me. Many times I was stranded without words. I've always admired Bill and other ministers who are able to produce at least three original sermons a week. The pressure of this must be terrific. The mixture of appreciation and criticism received makes each sermon an act of faith and courage.

During the time we were writing this we have continued to experience some trying times in our lives. Without sounding too pious I must tell you that God does not forsake us. He does answer the cries of our hearts when we turn the burden over to him and *wait*. We've been waiting a long time on some answers and little by little we see the answers coming—and not at all like we expected.

Something we need to add to the "How to Survive" chapter is *True Friends*. Friends who will stand with you through troubled times and happy times are part of God's loving touch. Being a friend and receiving friendship is a gift. It is easy to be bitter and question any offer of friendship or to grasp one or two people jealously. We need each other and in order to be able to give and receive friendship we must be open, caring, and patient. A *true friend* is a real treasure.

Remember that being stranded need not be devastating. You can survive. I know you will with God's help.